Awakening
to Change

Other books by Soozi Holbeche
published by Piatkus

The Power of Gems and Crystals
The Power of Your Dreams

Awakening to Change

A guide to self-empowerment
in the new millennium

SOOZI HOLBECHE

PIATKUS

With love

for Beinsa Douna, Brother Boris and Brother Krum, Big Maria, Marta
and Joanna, Helene, Danielle, Darinka, Jana, and everyone working for
change in Eastern Europe. With love to all who are pushed to the edge
and awaken to change. With especial love and appreciation to Desmond
who, despite his scepticism, encourages me anyway.

First published in 1993 by
Judy Piatkus (Publishers) Ltd of
5 Windmill Street, London W1P 1HF

Reprinted 1994

The moral right of the author has been asserted

A catalogue record for this book is
available from the British Library

ISBN 0-7499-1254-5

Edited by Martin Noble
Designed by Sue Ryall

The extract from *The Sleep of Prisoners*
is reproduced by permission of
Oxford University Press

Set in 11/13 pt Compugraphic Sabon
by Action Typesetting Ltd, Gloucester
Printed in Great Britain by
Bookcraft (Bath) Ltd

Come to the edge, he said.
They said: We are afraid.
Come to the edge, he said.
They came.
He pushed them ... and they flew.

GUILLAUME APOLLINAIRE

CONTENTS

Introduction   ix

Part One: Awakening to Change

1 Gateway to the future   3
2 Explosion of awareness   11
3 Symptoms of change   27
4 Following our own truths   38
5 Learning from the myths and prophecies of the past   48

Part Two: Ways Towards Inner Guidance

6 The healing power of thought   61
7 Using crystals for balance and vitality   75
8 Dreams as keys to empowerment   88
9 Honouring the Earth   100

Part Three: The Magic of Creative Living

10	Out of the shadows	123
11	Freedom from pain and fear	136
12	Into the next millennium	151
	Further reading	176
	Useful addresses	177
	Index	178

INTRODUCTION

The 1990s are a time of major planetary upheaval and cataclysmic change. It is as if the world and all the people in it are going through a dark night of the soul where nothing that used to work for us does so now in the same way. Relationships are breaking down, family life is falling apart; all over the world people are losing their jobs, homes, money, security. Politics, education and religion are in a state of flux. Earthquakes, floods, war and famine are causing havoc.

We are all suffering – the literal meaning of the word is 'to undergo' – a planetary near-death experience, stimulated by the Earth herself. By manifesting symptoms of disease, she forces us to look at our relationship with all of life.

Instead of wringing our hands at the apparent rise of chaos, disorder and conflict in the world I believe we should rejoice that all the ills are coming to the surface so that we can see what is confronting us. Without pain, discomfort, a lump or a rash, we remain unaware of the disease. When we experience its symptoms we do something about them.

These years are both a death and a birth, the ending of one civilisation and the beginning of another which in ancient China was known as Wei Chi. Wei Chi implies radical change, the midpoint between life and death, the moment of crisis in the delivery room when a woman is in labour and the baby has not yet emerged. It is also a time of great excitement – after all, parents delight in a birth. They do not focus on the pains of labour but plan for the future and the new life emerging.

It is a time of joy and celebration.

Maybe the pains of the changes moving across the face of the Earth are no more than the labour contractions of an expectant mother who knows exactly what she's doing – initiating us into another form of life. That she also knows the best way in which we can help is first to put our own lives in order and second to focus on the positive outcome of the new life emerging instead of the critical period of birth itself.

As Henry Miller once said, 'The world is not to be put in order, the world is order incarnate. It is for us to put ourselves in unison with this order.'

A leap into the future

I was six years old and, egged on by other children, climbed a wall so high that I was afraid to leap down from it. My mother appeared below me. Angry because I was late for supper, she yelled at me to jump down into her arms. I held back, afraid that she would not catch me, though I knew that I could not stay there forever. Eventually I was forced to jump. Many of us are like the child I once was. We cling to what appears to be safe and familiar. We know we cannot stay stuck forever, but we are afraid to let go, to jump into the unknown and move on.

One of our greatest fears is that of jumping into the unknown. We fear change. We fear insecurity, to lose control of the familiar. For us, change can stimulate feelings of uncertainty, fear and loneliness, pushing us to query many aspects of our existence – our careers, relationships, even the very quality of our lives.

However, it is through change that every one of us will have the opportunity to make a quantum leap into the future. This book explores ways of making this leap. It is for all of those who feel grave uncertainty about the world today, and are brave enough to try to do something about it.

All the exercises in the book are self-explanatory and easy to follow. I have used them many times in the last twenty-five years, in individual sessions and in groups. Use them, and allow yourself to move forward. Let understanding give you power.

Part One

AWAKENING
TO CHANGE

1

GATEWAY
TO THE FUTURE

We are living in very exciting times. According to historians, scientists, psychics, visionaries, environmentalists and indigenous peoples worldwide, it will be the most radical, dramatic and potent period of change in the planet's history. Almost everything we have known, valued and held on to is falling away to give birth to a new phase in human evolution as great as if we had stepped from water to land for the very first time. We are becoming part of a new species and a new culture.

The native American Indian Cherokee prophecies say that we are entering the ninth and final state of purification in which our consciousness must be transformed. In the process everything previously hidden must come to the surface.

The Mayan calendar also predicted that the years from 1987 to 2011 are and will be a time of purification. Edgar Cayce, known as the Sleeping Prophet and one of the world's greatest psychics, said in the 1930s, 'the transition will begin in those periods between 1958 and 1998. When this period has been accomplished then the New Era, the New Age, is to begin.' He added, 'Will you have a part in it or will you let it pass by and merely be a hanger-on?'

The 1990s are the gateway to the last phase of our present history. On every level huge changes are taking place which push us to move beyond the limitations of mass-conditioning selfishness, greed and competitiveness into an awareness of other worlds and our connection to them. A massive shift that will, in the future, make even the Industrial Revolution look small, is waking us from self to cosmic consciousness.

A dream of happiness

An aspect of this shift was foreshadowed in the 1960s when the catch-phrase of flower-power hippies was, 'All you need is love.'

That brief period of idealism in the 1960s symbolised a dream of happiness, fulfilment and sharing; a world where communities lived co-operatively; where nature and civilisation supported one another and where soul purpose and spiritual awareness prevailed. For many it was a new way forward, a Renaissance similar to that of the fifteenth century which resulted in an amazing burst of creative energy and a profound change in consciousness. For others it was a reactionary escape from materialism and a leap into the shimmery, illusionary glamour of psychicness; with the abnegation of personal responsibility that came from following a guru and doing exactly what he or she said – whether it was to wear purple, pink or orange clothes, become vegetarian or eat meat, shave heads or grow flowing, shoulder-length hair.

It was all part of a spiritual explosion but many outsiders reacted with fear and disapproval.

Although not a hippie I remember being involved with a community in America which was based around our mutual commitment to God, serving the planet as best as we knew how at the time and growing a garden.

Around this time Jim Jones and his followers in the remote jungles of Guyana all committed suicide. We had never even heard of him but from that time on we were considered to be a fanatical sect. Local churches preached about how evil we were and one Saturday morning a police car roared up and seized a two-year-old baby boy who was running around naked while his father watered the garden. We were accused of lewd, obscene behaviour and sexual deviation. Accusations were levelled at us from people who, despite many invitations to do so, never came to see for themselves what we were doing. Painting, building, planting trees, digging trenches, preparing the way for a bio-dynamic garden, we were far too busy and tired even to think of cavorting naked under the trees.

Their blind bigotry was similar to those people who would not look through Galileo's telescopes in case they had to admit that Copernicus was right when he said he could prove the Earth moved around the sun instead of the sun revolving around the Earth. Many people today have exactly the same resistance to change.

The guru teachers

The 1960s and 70s were very much the time of following the guru who could astral travel, pop into your room and take you on amazing out-of-body journeys, encourage you to explore sexuality on the understanding that unfulfilled desires would hold you back in the next life, or tap you with a feather to raise your kundalini and reach enlightenment. No wonder many students became entranced – a guru who can pop into your room and read your mind, appear and disappear through closed windows, doors or walls is more interesting than the college professor stuck in his study with his books.

The guru-teacher was right for a certain stage of evolution. However they nearly all taught that the most important teacher we can have is ourselves; the most valuable lesson we can learn is to go within.

In 1929 Krishnamurti, the man who was believed by the Theosophists to be the Avatar or world spiritual teacher, shocked his followers when he dissolved the 'Order of the Star', the organisation established to present him to the world. He challenged his listeners to awaken to the truth within themselves independent of any spiritual teacher or organisation.

Before Yogananda died he said it was now the end of the age of the guru and the time of fellowship. In the 1970s many teachers severed what were often emotionally addictive ties between themselves and their chelas, or students, by manifesting symptoms of imbalance and craziness.

In Australia a teacher appeared on stage with a brown paper bag completely enveloping his head. Turning his back on the audience and speaking through the paper bag, he said his vibrations were far too sensitive to expose them and proceeded to give his lecture, oblivious to the fact that three-quarters of his audience had left.

In South Africa another well-known seminar leader sat in front of a large group of enthusiastic followers with a bottle of whisky in one hand and a large can of sardines on his head. Helping himself to generous slurps from the bottle he spent three hours 'channelling the spirit of the sardines' (to say nothing of the spirit of the whisky).

Sexual scandals, bizarre behaviour rationalised as teaching devices, alcoholism, drug addiction, psychological exploitation, misuse of money and abuse of power – not just by charismatic New Age leaders but also by the Church and famous tele-evangelists – made big headlines and continued to do so into the 1980s. The amazement, shock or disappointment triggered by these antics catalysed people from dependency into discrimination; from an attitude towards the teacher of 'I'll give you my life, now take care of me', into 'I'll take care of myself'.

Most of us when we first discover books, teachings, people or philosophies which empower us to change our lives become like the baby who grabs, swallows, tastes and touches everything he can get his hands on. The sharper, the shinier, the more glittery, the better. Finally it's all too much and he wants to throw up. So do we – and we often need the jolt from the very person who inspired and initiated us into new thoughts and behaviour to do it.

Quest for the new

The early years of what we now call the New Age (coinciding with the time of the Punk movement when people wore safety pins in noses, ears and nipples), were a release from left-over Victorian prudery. There was a reaction to established institutions, to the floundering of the world economy and the rape of the environment. Nature began to show symptoms of toxicity but instead of paying attention most of humanity voted for more arms, bigger cars and increased factory production, and mocked the environmentalists who spoke of acid rain and the problems arising from hacking down trees and building roads through rain forests.

At the same time, many people, dissatisfied with material-ism, questioning old values and seeking a spiritual meaning to life, began to see that an immense change was afoot. There was a movement away from the city towards alternative lifestyles and community living. Small groups of people with similar beliefs, interests and questions began to come together. There was a ripple of excitement that in spite of nuclear problems and ecological imbalance the world was moving into a new phase.

This new phase included the thought that human self-sufficiency was not enough. Sir George Trevelyan, regarded as the father of the New Age in Britain, described this awakening of recognition to our relationship to the whole of life as:

> . . . the greatest revolution in the intellectual climate of human thought. We are discovering that this planet is not just a tiny unimportant speck in the universe, nor are we the only civilization. This earth is of paramount

importance as a channelling point through which spiritual being on all levels can flow and evolve. Humanity is to be seen as a great experiment of God going through the illusion of separation from the divineness and evolving self-consciousness to achieve conscious reintegration with the divine will, in free creativity, as co-creator and companion of God.

Findhorn: hard work and magic

The idea that Earth is a school and training ground for soul development is not new. The principle of brotherhood of man and the father/motherhood of God is common to many religions. However few people were able to grasp the concept that brotherhood included contact with the elemental world of nature spirits.

Two people who did were Peter and Eileen Caddy, founders of the Findhorn Community in Scotland. Sacked from his job of managing the Cluny Hotel in Forres, Scotland, Peter moved his family and secretary, Dorothy Maclean, into what he believed would be the temporary accommodation of a caravan, placed on an arid strip of sand at Findhorn bay in the north of Scotland. Assuming that he would soon resolve his difficulties with the hotel owners the family had to adjust to cramped quarters and lack of money which finally impelled them to grow their own vegetables.

These vegetables became a legend – fifty pound cabbages, roses in the snow, enormous carrots and tomatoes out of season. Yet when the soil was tested by the British Soil Association it was pronounced mostly sand and therefore 'dead' earth in which it should have been impossible to grow anything.

Pressed to explain how they did it Peter and Eileen described working from daily meditation and attunement to the devas – or angelic spirits – which animate the animal kingdom. During meditation Eileen also believed that she received specific guidance from God which was then acted upon by the group.

The results were virtually miraculous and led to hundreds of curious people coming to see for themselves what was going on. Many of them decided to stay and from these small beginnings the Findhorn community, now famous throughout the world, developed. Dorothy Maclean had a strong gift for devic/angelic communication herself and was as vital a part in the founding of Findhorn as were Peter and Eileen.

Many years later, at a Oneearth Conference in New Zealand, I was standing next to Dorothy when a woman rushed up to her and said, 'Quick, quick. Tell me about the Magic of Findhorn.'

Dorothy said, 'It was not magic – it was hard work.'

'No, no,' the woman replied. 'I want to know about the Magic.'

Again Dorothy repeated, 'It was not magic. It was very hard work!'

The woman recoiled, disgusted. 'You're just ordinary – I thought you were a special, magical person.' Dorothy quietly smiled and said, 'Yes, I am ordinary – and special and magic, just like you.'

All over the planet people were beginning to experiment with the magical and miraculous through meditation, mind expansion techniques and communication with higher streams of intelligence, including extra-terrestrial – as well as talking to trees, plants and machinery.

Those who thought that, by coming together in small groups, holding hands and 'letting go and letting God', was all they had to do soon found that letting go to God was hard work, just as Dorothy Maclean said. It meant action, discipline, putting lives in order physically, emotionally, mentally and spiritually. Many groups fell by the wayside but it was still a time of spiritual awakening, a realisation that we are more than our merely physical senses and that, in the words of F. C. Happold:

*A wind has blown across the world, and tremors shake its
frame.*
*New things are struggling to their birth and nought shall be
the same.*
The earth is weary of its past of folly, hate and fear,
Beyond the dark and stormy sky, the dawn of God is near.

2

EXPLOSION OF AWARENESS

In the 1980s these winds of change blew more intensely through the world, opening previously closed windows in people's minds, blowing away the cobwebs of old thoughts, traditions and ideals. It was like switching on a light in a previously dark room where people asleep began to wake up and take a long hard look at the world around them. There was a revulsion against war, killing and violence reflected in films such as *Apocalypse Now*, *The Killing Fields* and *Platoon*.

The green movement initiated a new awareness into the damage we were doing to the environment. Acid rain, holes in the ozone layer, global warming, millions of trees destroyed to provide land for cattle and paper production, many animal species decimated to the point of extinction and exhaust fumes poisoning the atmosphere, all of these things shocked us into acknowledging the relationship between over-consumption and the pollution of the Earth around us. Hundreds of people responded to earthquakes, hurricanes, changing weather patterns, disease, famine and population explosion by taking steps to become self-sufficient. Alternative technology, vegetarianism, organic and bio-dynamic farming became the order of the day. Others reacted in fear, dread for the future, confusion over the complexity of the problems faced and, ignoring the screams of the Earth to make us listen, continued to pollute and rape the planet.

A polarisation began to take place between people excited and optimistic that this was a period of cleansing, and an opportunity to move forward into a new era, and those fearing catastrophe and the end of the world. In the words of Sun Bear, a native American and founder of the Bear Tribe Medicine Society, whom I was fortunate to meet and spend time with:

> I see that many humans are not yet willing to make the necessary changes in themselves and their actions which could prevent the most severe consequences. They will not stop polluting, they will not stop consuming the Earth's resources as if those gifts were theirs alone; they will not stop acting towards nature and all her creatures – including other humans – as if they were only a back-drop for their activities. They simply will not learn to walk in a sacred manner on the earth.

My own quantum leap

While prophets of doom avidly read Nostradamus and predicted the imminent arrival of the Anti-Christ (someone who causes humanity harm), war and global destruction – and others forecast the rebirth of the Christ energy into the Earth and the advent of the Aquarian Age – my life was full of excitement, adventure and spiritual expansion.

I had grown up with a psychic sensitivity which enabled me to see what people thought (which often did not match what they said!). I saw past, present and future simultaneously, would say things and they happened, have conversations with invisible beings whom I could see as lines of energy, or shadowy forms like the negative of a black and white photo.

I often saw through walls, ceilings, tables and chairs. So called 'solid matter' used to disintegrate into vibrating atoms and I was aware of the consciousness of life-force, in everything around me. It was like an on/off switch in my brain that could suddenly catapult me into a totally different perception of reality.

I sometimes put my hands around ailing plants or people in pain and felt an energy, a heat, pouring through me which often helped them. We all have these capacities but at that time, knowing nothing of senses beyond seeing, touching, hearing, speaking and feeling, I became a little afraid.

As a child I soon learned that these were not experiences to talk about. If I did I was accused of lying, pretending or having too vivid an imagination.

I tried to cut these inner senses off until the day that illness, accident, constant crisis and disaster impelled me to scream at God, 'The only thing that has not happened in my life is that the ceiling has not fallen on my head.' As I spoke the ceiling crumbled and fell, knocking lamps off tables and pictures from walls. In shock I asked, 'What do you want me to do?' A voice rang through the room, 'Meditate' and so meditate I did.

Meditation transformed my life, put me in touch with a wiser, more honest part of myself, that helped me to trust and use the awareness that previously seemed like a curse. Dreams, always a strong part of my life, increased in power and clarity. In one I found myself rushing through space to hang on the moon looking back at the planet (almost like Edgar Mitchell, whose vision of the Earth at the time of the moon-landing changed his life), while a voice said, 'You have to make a quantum leap in consciousness. You think you've done so before but it is nothing in comparison to what you must do in the future.'

Part of my quantum leap was to stop doing anything I did not believe in. Ideas that life was meant to consist solely of earning a living, getting married, owning a house, a car, having X amount of money in the bank, two or three weeks' holiday a year, before retirement and waiting for death, fell away. So did material possessions.

Instead of working in fashion and design I spent my time with accident victims, cancer patients and the terminally ill. I was so poor that when the soles of my shoes disintegrated and my clothes began to fall apart I was delighted to receive cast-offs from concerned friends. I learned that when you do what you believe — the word means I be-live: I live what I believe — the universe co-operates. All my needs were met.

Wanting to meet Elizabeth Kubler Ross, the well-known Swiss psychiatrist and physician, a ticket for America arrived through the post from an anonymous donor, with a small note attached saying, 'I had a feeling you'd like to go.' Secretly dreaming of Sri Lanka and the elephants of my childhood I suddenly received a gift in the form of a five-week holiday in Sri Lanka. I saw the house where I had lived, joined the elephants for the Temple of the Tooth procession in Kandy (an annual procession in celebration of the Buddha's losing a tooth when he visited the island hundreds of years ago), and watched extraordinary acupuncture operations where, with only needles behind the ears and in between the thumbs and forefingers, a 25 lb goitre was removed, a Caesarean birth and brain surgery took place. Money for an operation I needed but could not afford came literally out of the blue. A dress I'd admired appeared on my doorstep. It was almost as if I only had to think of something and it materialised.

I discovered books, magazines and organisations which helped me understand that much of what I had experienced in childhood was quite normal. An eclectic range of authors from Herman Hesse, George Gurdjieff, Suzuki, Christmas Humphreys, Alan Watts, Alice Bailey, Ram Dass, Thomas Mann, Idries Shah and many many others, expanded my thinking. The Sufi books by Hazarat Inayat Khan became my bible. I studied astrology, numerology, the tarot and the I-Ching. I learned about Uri Geller and Matthew Manning's telekinetic powers, which attracted world-wide attention when tested by scientists, explored Kirlian photography, reincarnation, the Kabbalah, astral travel and life after death.

I felt as if I had been living in a box and suddenly the lid was removed. I jumped out into a new and wonderful world where I was surrounded by people who had made their own quantum leap into a completely new way of looking at life; people who had not only had similar experiences to mine and felt free to discuss them but who also wanted to explore them further.

The sleeping giant wakes up

As my healing practice began to develop I was invited to Australia, America, Kenya, South Africa and many European countries to give lectures and seminars. No matter where I went, whether I spent time with western educated or indigenous people, I saw the same things happening, as if, to quote Jean Houston, 'a sleeping giant was waking up and slowly stretching in the hearts and minds of millions'. The idea of what it was to be a human being was starting to expand.

Increasingly the stereotyped male – female roles changed. Men, embodying a more feminine energy than in the past, became more willing to show their feelings. Women, flexing a few unused muscles, began to stand up, assert and express themselves in a way previously considered masculine. In fact the 1960s women's movement began with women stepping out to claim their power. Now, in the 1990s men are stepping in to rediscover their feelings, imagination and intuition.

In an Australian magazine I read an article (by Alan Lowen) entitled 'Male ego, the longest running show on the planet'. It went on to say:

Male ego has been running the show for a long time. It really knows how to look after itself. Yet really it is nothing more than armouring. For some strange reason, I guess in order to 'civilise the world' man decided a few thousand years ago that he needed to take the controls. Something in women must have frightened him, because in the process he started to use his power to suppress the female spirit in woman, in himself and in the world. He learned to feel less and to care less. Gradually he came to identify himself with his thickening skin, and to lose touch with the deeper mysteries of his being.

His armour protected him from himself. His hardening and deadening affected his children, passed on from generation to generation through both men and women. It is true that there are many women whose female spirit has been anaesthetised by male conditioning, including some feminists who are as oppressive as some of their male counterparts. (The same happened in the reverse under the power of the Amazonian matriarchy.)

This deadening of, and disconnection from, warmth and feeling, is what enables men and women to abuse their children, violate each other or fight bloody wars based on an inflexible belief that their way is the only way and in which people are tortured to death for having a different point of view.

It is like a blindness, symbolised by a children's story I once read in which an old man is going blind and lame. He spends his days bemoaning the fact that he has three daughters instead of sons. Repeatedly he says, 'If only I had a son he would have the strength and courage to fetch the medicine to heal me from the doctor on the other side of the mountain.' Finally, after many adventures and much effort, it is the daughters who get him to walk and to see. The story reflects the blindness of the man, or male ego (which as we have seen, can affect women as much as men) who, unable to recognise the value of feeling, imagination and intuition (the three sisters), indifferent to love and compassion, trusting only left-brain logic and the idea of masculine superiority (which boils down to the ability to do rather than to be), ceases to relate to life as it is.

This refusal to see and participate in what is real around him cuts him off. He becomes an emotional cripple. The old man's revival comes through acknowledging the power of the feminine, the power of intuitive right-brain as well as left-brain thinking which, when aligned with the masculine (the daughters put on male clothing to accomplish their task), brings about healing and balance.

Another part of the story describes how the doctor's son accompanies the third daughter, who he thinks is a boy, through the mountains when she takes the medicine back to her father. It is a journey of many days and on the way they become friends. Once home the girl takes off her disguise and instead of being shocked the doctor's son is delighted. It is a bonus to discover that his travelling companion is female. He marries her and, like all good fairy-tales, they live happily ever after.

As the patriarchal domination of the world comes to an end, and the armour mentioned by Alan Lowen melts, men and women, tired of the conflict created by mutual attack and defence games, are becoming friends and companions – equals – seeking intimacy rather than hostility. Role-swapping, in the sense of women going to work and men staying at home to look after the children, is now quite common, whereas a few years ago it was considered peculiar. It is a move towards becoming more conscious, loving human beings instead of aggressively male or female.

Giving up one's baggage

During my travels I worked, met and lived with hundreds of people who had broken some invisible barrier, crossed a frontier into a country where everything was possible. To do this the old identity had to be dropped, as if the passports to cross this frontier were no longer valid. Ironically this truth was about to be driven home to me only too uncomfortably.

In fact no sooner had I had this thought about passports

suddenly losing their potency than I found myself travelling in Europe, giving seminars on meditation, dreams, journal-writing, stress release, crystals and healing.

One day, on a train between Holland and Germany, the police asked for my passport and, having seen it, said they wanted further proof of my identity. As I planned only one night in Germany to see friends before travelling to America to attend a cancer conference I was travelling light. So light I only had a handbag and toothbrush with me – even my plane tickets were in Amsterdam.

Refusing to accept this the police took me off the train and put me in a cell in the local police station, from where they said they would call the foreign office in London. I opened my bag to read an article by Jerry Jampolski, whom I was to introduce at the cancer conference and found the headlines: 'Have you ever felt lonely, unloved and depressed? Have you ever felt locked up, pushed in a corner where you cannot get out?' I closed my eyes and said, 'God, why is this happening to me?' When I opened my eyes a few minutes later I saw on a bench in the opposite corner the book *I Never Promised You a Rose Garden*. It seemed a pretty direct answer to my question.

Three days later, with the help of the local British consul, and having missed my original plane, I arrived in New York. Ecstatic to be out of the police cell and standing on the free, welcoming shores of America, I presented my passport to the control. Two seconds later a heavy hand fell on my shoulder and, categorised as an undesirable alien, I was marched off for what turned out to be a long and intense interrogation.

'Who are you? What do you do?' I was asked by a burly, uniformed man. Thinking that stress-release sounded less airy-fairy than meditation I replied, 'I teach stress-release'. He gazed at me while opening my suitcase, strewing its contents over the counter between us. My appointment diary lay on the top of the pile and picking it up he read a poem I'd copied out of a recipe book which began, 'I want to live to be an outrageous old woman and not an old lady. I want to have ten thousand lovers in one love.'

He missed the first two lines, as well as the words 'in one love' and ran a finger along, to 'I want to have ten thousand lovers.' Incredulous he said, 'You call this stress-release? We have another name for it here.'

I was doomed. I had money of different denominations from the workshops I'd given in different European countries which was going to a community in America, together with notes, most of them still unread, saying things like 'My few hours with you have changed my life.' No matter how hard I tried to prove myself — showing the invitations to lecture, the temporary visa that indicated I was not planning to stay — nor what I said, he would not move an inch from the idea of the ten thousand lovers and what that implied to him.

Suddenly a gun went off. I leaped back and looked round to see a man in Arab clothes lying on the floor in a pool of blood. Sick with shock, as if the strings holding my bones together had been cut, I watched the room fill with uniformed men. Doctors, nurses, ambulance men and a stretcher appeared. After what seemed an eternity and much discussion, the man was removed.

'Why did you do that?' I asked.

'It was him or us,' was the reply. 'Besides, we only shoot to wound, not to kill.'

They turned their attention back to me. 'Now who are you, really?' To explain their ferocity, months later I discovered that the German police had alerted New York because they suspected I was part of the Baader-Meinhof Gang.

Having spent five hours — and three days before this — trying to prove who I was, I suddenly felt it was irrelevant and did not matter.

'I am,' I answered.

'You're what?'

'I am.'

'What does that mean, I am?'

'I just am. I have nothing else to say.'

He shrugged, repacked my suitcase, handed it to me and let me go. I realised that as soon as I dropped all desire to prove or explain myself, let go of who I thought I was or ought to be, life moved on again.

Movements of awareness

Across the globe hundreds of others were also discovering and expressing new, true identities. In England, the Findhorn Foundation, the Wrekin Trust founded by Sir George Trevelyan, and the Festival for Mind, Body and Spirit started by Graham Wilson in 1977, introduced people to ideas that seemed so way out that the press deemed the festival a collection of cranks.

Graham conceived the idea after trying to find for himself answers to questions about religion, philosophy, astrology and numerous other subjects. He realised other people probably had similar questions and so, hiring Olympia – normally used for shows such as the Ideal Home Exhibition – he gathered together a vast array of people and information. In order to pay for this Graham mortgaged his house, so strong was his belief in his idea of the Festival.

Olympia was filled with the sounds of hundreds of people experimenting with yoga, dowsing, aura reading, telepathy, UFO discoveries, teaching the blind to see through developing inner or psychic senses, dance, vegetarianism, clairvoyance, Tai Chi, reincarnation, philosophy, religion, mind-control, spiritual healing, meditation, and psychic sciences such as palm and tarot reading, to name but a few. They learned about crystals, kinesiology, whole-food, planetary chakras, Kirlian photography, ley lines, herbal remedies, massage, water-births, aromatherapy, standing stones, pyramidology and the secret life of plants.

At one festival there was a greenhouse which monitored the plants' reaction to people passing by. At another hundreds danced around a maypole before having their hands, heads or hearts read through psychic readings, which often included a drawing of their spirit guide. Some came to buy a stick of incense and found new meaning and purpose to life. Others came out of curiosity or to meet a friend. All discovered a thousand and one different routes to self-fulfilment and understanding from baking organic bread to healing a faltering relationship. Even the cloakroom attendants commented on the atmosphere in which not one child cried or got lost and people were happy and smiling.

Newspaper reporters who had initially poured scorn on the festival, came back to find mile-long queues of people waiting to get in, and started to write, 'Maybe 100,000 people can't be wrong. Something is going on.'

The Wrekin Trust and the Festival for Mind, Body and spirit, made available to the general public people like Paul Solomon, sometimes called the modern Edgar Cayce; Hans Selye, a specialist in stress and ageing problems; Norman Cousins, former editor of the *New Yorker* who wrote the book *Anatomy of an Illness* after healing a supposedly incurable disease with carefully prescribed doses of laughter; Admiral Shattock who, despite advice to have surgery, healed an arthritic hip with mind power and visualisation. Indian gurus such as Muktenanda and Rajneesh were extremely popular and Sai Baba, whose teaching is based on the oneness between God and creation, drew hundreds of followers to his ashram in India to see for themselves the sacred ash (or Vibhuti) and jewels he produced out of the air. Numerous healers such as Rose Gladden, Andrew Watson and many many more, demonstrated the transference of mental and physical energy in healing.

Close Encounters of the Third Kind, the *Star Wars* series, later followed by *E.T.*, opened people's minds to the possibility of UFOs and extra-terrestrial communication. I remember going to the press showing of *Close Encounters* before it hit the general cinema route and the whole audience of 'seen it all before' entertainment critics rose to their feet and clapped. Films on reincarnation such as *Heaven Can Wait*, followed later by *Field of Dreams*, *Dead Again*, *Truly Madly Deeply*, *Ghost* and *Always* – together with television and news articles on near-death experience – reflected the changing awareness and interests sweeping through people's minds.

As impressive an opening to this new awareness was Findhorn, mentioned in the previous chapter. Starting off as an apparent giant vegetable-growing experiment it has become a community of people devoted to personal development and healing the planet. Initially based on Eileen's guidance from God, it gradually expanded to each person learning to trust their own guidance, and take responsibility for themselves and the community. Whether a person came for two weeks or five years their lives were profoundly changed. Many have taken what they learned back into their own countries and communities and inspired others as Peter and Eileen Caddy inspired them.

I went to Findhorn expecting magic and was put to work on maintenance – cleaning out blocked loos or scrubbing bricks – and otherwise cooking in the kitchen. I learned that work was love in action and that total acceptance by others of who we are, in the moment, can catalyse complete change. I found that every nook and cranny of garden, hotel (the community finally took over the Cluny hotel from which Peter had been fired), community building and caravans reflected the love and attention put into them. The flowers seemed more colourful, the people taller, brighter and shinier than outside the community and even the machinery – whether for garden, house or kitchen – operated cheerfully in response to being thanked. Everyone and everything was treated with respect and care.

Despite, or maybe because of, cleaning blocked loos and scrubbing bricks, I had some extraordinary spiritual experiences. Whether meditating in the Sanctuary or simply sitting outside on the grass I frequently felt hands rest on my shoulders and then had a sense of liquid gold being poured into my body through the top of my head to the tips of my toes. I felt every cell in my body tingle and glow. For days afterwards whatever I touched sparked as if a match had been struck.

I climbed mountains in Bulgaria and discovered a brotherhood, with whom I am still involved, who showed me the meaning of truth, purity and simplicity in spiritual development. Their work, based on the teachings of Beinsa Douna, sometimes known as Peter Deunov, encourages the same principles as Findhorn of love, work and spiritual discipline. Beinsa Douna's work, which emphasised love of God and union with God, had its source in the Orphic mysteries of Thrace (now Bulgaria) which flowed through Pythagoras and Plato into esoteric Christianity, through the Essenes and Christian Gnostics, through the Bogomils and Cathars – both of which movements called themselves the friends of God. He had at least 40,000 followers before the war and, as a result of the greater freedom in the East since the apparent collapse of Communism, his teaching is now re-emerging.

For me to camp and climb in Bulgaria, waking at 4 a.m. to greet the rising sun, dancing the series of meditational movements of paneurhythmy, set to music and words composed by Beinsa Denov himself, to be surrounded by the extraordinary atmosphere of the Rila mountains and the sense of the presence of this great teacher, was like a living meditation. I had experiences of shrinking to a grain of sand and expanding to include the whole universe. I had visions of great spiritual presence, beings of light pouring energy into the Earth which I saw as a violet ray of transformation, bringing changes which were not always comfortable. Each visit transformed and healed me.

Time seemed to be speeding up both horizontal and vertical time – inner and outer – as if civilisation had started on the outside edge of a long-playing gramophone record and, like a gramophone needle speeds up as it moves from the wider circumference to the narrower bit near the hole in the middle, was now spinning faster. We are finishing a phase of evolution and getting read to plop through the 'hole in the middle' and start the next phase.

Entering the void

Individually many people have gone into this hole which can give a sense of void or being in limbo. The void can be black, like the dark night of the soul, which rips away the fabric and foundation of our lives, moves us from breakdown to breakthrough. The phrase 'dark night of the soul' comes from writings of the Spanish mystic, St John of the Cross. Today it implies the crisis when the things that used to work for us no longer do. If we find ourselves in a dark void we need to remember that a seed grows buried in dark soil. It needs the dark to germinate and bring forth new life.

It can also be a white void in which there is a sense of excitement that something is about to happen, even if we are not sure yet what it will be; it is like coming to a crossroads where there is no sign and we wait to see what to do next.

It is a major initiation. The biggest mistake is to do nothing. Many of us recognise this but are so afraid of making a mistake we sit glued to our seats waiting for the hand of God to drop out of the sky with a sign to make everything clear. Instead of doing nothing we should get in touch with our inner guide through meditation, visualisation and dreams as I suggest in chapters 6 and 8. If we listen to our inner wisdom we shall discover there are no mistakes but simply a variety of experiences to choose from.

Opening ourselves up to change

The consciousness of the planet is lifting to another level as if the chakras of the Earth were opening and expanding. Chakra in Sanskrit means 'wheel' and each chakra in the human body is a whirring vortex of energy, vibrating at different frequencies. The lowest three chakras vibrate at a lower frequency than do the heart, throat, third eye and crown chakra. As the heart chakra of the Earth expands – which has been happening for the last 30–40 years, as we move into the fourth dimension and prepare for the fifth, we experience the vibrational frequency of the planet speeding up, a sense of accelerated change.

If we can move with this acceleration life can be full of excitement; if not we'll experience fear, panic and life in chaos while we adjust to it. It can also produce uncomfortable physical, mental and emotional side effects which I will discuss in the next chapter.

No matter whether these past years have inspired us to change voluntarily, or because life fell apart through loss of job, health or relationship, the Great Earth Mother on which we live is shaking us awake, forcing us to put our lives in order and take note of what is going on around us. In the process we have to clear our emotional bodies which, like soggy sponges, have absorbed everything that has ever happened to us – from this and other lives. Whether it be re-birthing, co-counselling, past-life therapy or any of the myriad other forms of help, the techniques made available to us during the past 30–40 years are carefully designed to aid us. So are some of the life situations that squeeze our emotional bodies dry, thus enabling us finally to act rather than react, live rather than just survive.

By thinking differently – by acting instead of reacting – we can tap into limitless creativity, infinite possibilities. In fact these years have been pushing us all to stand up and act rather than react.

A few years ago I was in Los Angeles and met a man who knew Emmet Fox, the writer and philosopher, when he first arrived in America. He told me this story about Emmet's first visit to a self-service restaurant.

Never having been in one before, he sat and waited to be served, becoming increasingly impatient at being unable to attract the attention of a waiter or waitress, and even more so when he realised that other people who came in after him were now sitting in front of steaming plates of food.

Finally, thoroughly exasperated, he got up and approached a man at a nearby table and said: 'I've been sitting here for twenty minutes without anyone taking a bit of notice. Now I see that you, who came in five minutes ago, sit here with a complete meal in front of you. What's going on? How do you get served in this country?'

The man, astonished, replied: 'But this is a self-service restaurant!' He pointed to the far end of the room where food was abundantly displayed. 'Go over there, take a tray, choose exactly what you want, pay for it, then sit down and eat it!'

Feeling a little silly, Emmet Fox followed the man's instructions and, as he put the food on the table, it suddenly struck him that life itself was a self-service restaurant. All manner of events, opportunities, situations, joys, delights and sadnesses are set out before us, and most of us remain fixed, bottoms glued to our seats, so busy looking at what everyone else has on their plates, wondering, 'Why has he got jelly and ice-cream? Why has she got a bigger helping?' that it never occurs to us simply to get up, see what is available, and choose what we want. When we do, to quote Sun Bear again, 'we will realise the generous and loving nature that is ours just as it is a part of all creation'.

3

SYMPTOMS
OF CHANGE

In the massive shift which is taking place on every level of existence, from planetary to sub-atomic, many of us are experiencing great discomfort. Across the world for the past twenty years, I saw, and still see, the same symptoms coming up: chronic, glandular-fever type tiredness in which people feel so droopy that they can hardly put one foot in front of another; the sense of time speeding by so fast that there is never enough time – even children feel this.

To live in the fourth dimension means we have 20 per cent less time and everything takes 20 per cent more time to do, so it is essential to focus on priorities. For example, stop dusting or cleaning the car every day and write the book you always wanted to write, or read one someone else wrote that can expand your consciousness.

In the story of Psyche and Aphrodite one of Psyche's tasks was to sort the seeds of the world. This also means the need to sort priorities, learning when to say yes and when to say no, especially if saying yes affects our ability to do what we came here to do.

Relationships

This loss of time can also induce a feeling of losing control of one's life. 'Not only are my relationships falling apart but I can no longer keep my cupboards and drawers tidy. Everything is in chaos from kitchen to office-desk.' Relationships are increasingly difficult to sustain because we have got to become whole and secure within ourselves without being totally dependent on someone else.

The average marriage or relationship starts off with a scenario something like this. I, Jane, not feeling too sure of myself, am delighted to be invited out. I put on my best clothes and best behaviour. Because I am insecure, a few outings down the line I am unconsciously going to show my date/admirer how awful I believe I am. I throw a tantrum. He either recoils and disappears from my life or shrugs, thinks I am in a strange mood but our apparent previous compatibility merits hanging in there. I am initially relieved but then – again unconsciously – think, 'If I'm so awful and he thinks I'm OK he can't be so hot himself.'

I begin in various ways, big and small, to treat him with contempt. He in turn does the same to me. I also show him what buttons he can press in me by my reactions to what he does and says. If we do not feel secure in ourselves we end up in unhealthy situations of button-pushing – which gives us a false sense of power – while propping each other up in between.

Instead of looking outside for what we need from someone else, we must look within. The collapse even of loving, supportive relationships now push many men and women to do just that. If we stop projecting on to the people around us, our own imbalance – or lack of empathy with our own inner male and female – which usually comes from poor relationships with our parents, life can change dramatically.

Sexuality

Men and women are becoming androgynous – a combination of male and female, with neither predominant. As a result our views of sex are also changing. These views are conditioned by the society in which we live. The Victorians were so prudish and overtly fearful of seduction that they not only wore three or four layers of clothing in bed but also covered the legs of the tables from which they ate. In contrast Rome, under Caligula, showed the most arrant licentiousness and sexual cruelty. In Greece the practice by the élite – especially in Plato's time – of homosexuality, combined with the social duty of marriage, was completely normal. Currently ideal sex should include body, mind, spirit and feeling. The problems we may now have about sex are not about sex itself but how we think about sex.

If you or I grew up in a family where it was totally acceptable to run around naked or to see our parents naked, we are likely to be far more comfortable with our own bodies and therefore our sexuality. The way in which we first learn about sex can also affect our attitude to it. When she was seven years old one of my patients was told by her mother, in response to a question about sex (having overheard the word in the school toilet), 'Never go near a Chinese man, they breed like rabbits.' This was the sum total of her sex education. A few months later, going to see a friend who lived in a block of flats, she found herself in a lift with a Chinese man. She shrank away from him but for two or three years afterwards was both terrified, and convinced, that she was pregnant. She had absolutely no knowledge of what happened to cause pregnancy.

A friend, sent to a Catholic boarding school, was indoctrinated with the idea that even to see another girl naked was a mortal sin. These were eight- and nine-year-old children. Another friend, male, given the same message by the brothers at his school, became traumatised by the memory of seeing the three-year-old sister of a friend naked in her bath. This, he was told, damned him to eternal hellfire. He was about ten years old at the time. This kind of indoctrination can (although not always of course) lead to sexual impotence or 'furtive sex' in the sense of secret titillation from nudity, whether on the beach or through pornographic magazines and clubs.

Human sexuality is based on the desire to commune with or be at one with another person (you and I are one). It is a communication underneath which is the desire to be at one with God. Whether we love each other, animals, our environment or crystals and stones, it is all part of the same instinctive desire for oneness. Therefore, however love comes, we need to celebrate it.

Sexuality leads us towards enlightenment. Passion is part of compassion: you cannot have one without the other. I read recently that sexual energy is 'close' to spiritual energy. I do not believe there is a difference. There is the undifferentiated energy of the universe which we use for running, talking, walking, baking a cake or making love. It is the energy of creation. We should not repress it but instead decide, or be aware of, how we channel it.

Homosexuality, confusion and guilt

Human love is not a substitute for spiritual love but an aspect of it. In this sense homosexuality is as relevant as any other kind of loving. It is based on the same instinctive desire for oneness. A few years ago much of my work involved homosexuality. This included both men and women who had sex change operations.

Homosexuality combines confusion – 'I feel female in a male body' or vice versa – with the need to reinforce male or female energy, which may have been missing since childhood, as well as a refusal to deal with the spiritual lessons chosen for this life. In every case there was a pattern of guilt and lack of self-acceptance.

John Bradshaw, a counsellor who specialises in family therapy, describes this pattern as a 'toxic shame'. 'Toxic shame' is the feeling of being flawed and defective as a human person, whether male or female.

Guilt says: 'I *made* a mistake.' 'Toxic shame' says: 'I *am* a mistake.'

This shame affects, to some degree or another, 98 per cent of humanity and is a major contributing cause of our massive addiction problems as well as unhealthy relationships with each other. It is imperative to recognise and heal this wound, much of which comes from family training that encourages us to repress emotion and not say how we really feel.

To change sex on the outside will not automatically change how we feel on the inside. One of my sex-change clients, now a woman having previously been a husband, and father of an eleven-year-old daughter, was still desperately unhappy and insecure three years after the operation. In the middle of a particularly traumatic and difficult session I suddenly heard the sound of laughter fill the room.

I looked up and had a vision of a group of hierarchical beings standing around helpless with mirth at how seriously, and guiltily, we deal with our sexuality. I saw an image of humanity as two- and three-year-old children playing in a sandpit with no clothes on and exploring their differences – which, after all, we have been given to explore. I realised that our teachers and guides look on our antics in the same way we would our own two- and three-year-old children. Also that the only 'sin' – the word in Greek means 'to miss the mark' – is to deliberately hurt or harm another.

Sharing this vision with my client had a far more profound effect than any 'proper' therapy. She is now getting on with the rest of her life having dropped the baggage of her past.

Releasing relationships with love

Relationships, whether with men or women, are to speed our growth. We are attracted to the person or people who will create change within us. Like a mirror image they reflect parts of us we may not recognise without them. This means we come together not necessarily to stay together but to grow.

31

When we have learned what we needed to learn, maybe it is time to move on. If we could have an attitude of 'we will use this relationship to serve our mutual need to be whole', and release it with love when it no longer serves that purpose, the ending of relationships – whether with job, family, lover, house or country – would be far less painful. I do not mean we should abandon our commitments without any attempt to sort out problems. However, we live in a world vastly different from that of our grandparents.

In the current climate of change it may not be possible, or even beneficial for our soul's growth, to stay with one person for sixty or seventy years. Perhaps families of the future will consist of small groups of like-minded people who together contract to bring up children with an option to move on when their task is finished. This might well provide more emotional intimacy than much of our so-called family life today.

We have chosen this life

No matter what happens in the future, we must understand that the purpose of life is spiritual growth. That no thing – person, situation, accident or illness – comes into our lives by mistake. Everything has been carefully chosen; everything that we have set in motion we will meet again, not as punishment but in order to understand the laws of cause and effect. We wrote a script which we then produced, directed and acted in. We chose our parents as well as many of the problems we now complain about.

In fact the people who have been the most difficult and un-lovable are probably the ones who love us the most. For example, before coming to Earth I may recognise that I had a previous life as a tyrant and bully. I now decide to experience what it feels like to be on the receiving end of this treatment. I run around saying to members of my soul family, or other friends: 'I have to go to Earth again and live out another life. Please would one of you play the part of a bullying, arrogant father?'

Most of them say: 'No – we have other things to do.' Again and again I ask. Finally someone says: 'Well, I do not want to do it, but because I love you and know it will help you to evolve and grow, I will.' This entity descends into the Earth plane. I later become his daughter and, when he bullies me, bemoan my fate. 'Why me? Why do I have to suffer like this?', completely forgetting that I created the situation in the first place.

Conception, birth and self-worth

Not only do we choose our parents but we also participate in the moment of our conception. Our consciousness enters the auric field of the mother six weeks before she conceives. The attitude of the man and woman (who ultimately become our parents) to each other, both sexually and emotionally, in that moment affect our acceptance or rejection of our own male and female qualities.

We identify with it, good, bad or indifferent – which affects our self-worth as well as our ability to enjoy sex. The attitude of the woman at the moment of knowing she is pregnant – not by intuition or imagination, but by the physical fact of the doctor telling her this is so – also affects our self-acceptance and identity. If I, as the mother, am either unmarried, unprepared or pregnant for the nineteenth time, I might say, 'Oh, *no*! It's too soon, too late or too much.' If the soul coming in identifies with this reaction – in other words, 'I am the cause of fear, unhappiness and resistance' – it will inevitably feel guilty and unworthy.

Future generations must learn the spiritual significance of conception, birth and early childhood. Meanwhile, if we gave more attention to babies and children when they are laughing and happy, and less when they scream and behave badly, we would begin to sow seeds of – 'I matter more when I am happy than when I am sad.' This in turn would help change our unconscious adult patterns of sometimes becoming sick to draw attention to ourselves when we feel unloved and depressed.

Change and dis-ease

Depression, apprehension, vague feelings of dis-ease, as well as any confusion arising from the break-up of family life and relationships as we have known them, are also common symptoms of the changes we are moving through.

Our immune system is breaking down and we are suffering, like the Earth, from an overdose of toxicity. Cancer, together with AIDS and TB – now becoming as much of a problem as AIDS – are symbolic of the Earth's problems. Cancer is basically a 'selfish' disease. One cell eats another and then another and so on until it finally kills the host on which it lives. Is it not similar to what mankind is doing to the Earth?

AIDS, among other things, produces lesions in the skin. The Earth has lesions caused by industrial pollution, nuclear poisoning, acid rain, ozone layer depletion and deforestation – which causes non-arable land and desert.

TB is a disease of the lungs. The trees are the lungs of the Earth and what do we do but cut them down without adequate replacement? Some cultures, such as the Japanese, use the equivalent of a forest a day in disposable chopsticks. We also fill the atmosphere with carbon dioxide from the cars we drive so neither we nor the trees can breathe properly. The collapse of our immune system can also be seen in the increasing number of people – again world-wide – suffering from chronic bronchitis, pneumonia, sinusitis, allergies, coughs, colds and 'flu that will not go away. Others have cramplike pains in the bones and joints, continual sore throats, teeth, mouth and neck problems.

We are presently at the mid-point between death of the old and birth of the new. We have a choice between standing still and clinging to the apparent safety of the past or taking the risk of leaping forward into the unknown. Part of us says, 'Yes, I'll jump,' but another part panics and says, 'But maybe this means I'll have to leave home, job, family.' This unconscious fear grabs us by the throat – which is where we give birth to a new identity, a new expression of ourselves –

which in turn leads to mouth, throat and chest problems.

Allergies are also on the increase. Not just allergies to certain foods or pollens in the air but also to synthetic fabrics. During a residential workshop in New Zealand the participants switched roles for a day. This included swopping clothes. A doctor who always wore pure cotton, after wearing the synthetic blouse, jumper and skirt belonging to her partner, became depressed and developed a chronic migraine headache. She was so sick she spent the next day in bed.

Trying to discover the cause, we suddenly realised the only difference had been in the clothes she had been wearing. We muscle-tested her, using the technique of kinesiology, or Touch for Health as it is often called, and found that she was definitely allergic to anything synthetic. (I wrote about this technique in my crystal book. There are many good books available which describe in detail how to use it.) We also muscle-tested the owner of the clothes and found she was allergic to what she wore too! She told us she nearly always felt tired and depressed and, while not exactly ill, frequently found it hard to complete a day's work. She gradually replaced her easy-care synthetic clothes with natural fibre and since then has never looked back.

I am not suggesting that everyone is necessarily allergic to what is not pure and natural. I am suggesting that it is a good idea to check that what you are doing to your body, inside and out, promotes optimum health and well-being. We are all far more sensitive than we used to be, partly due to build-up of toxicity in ourselves and everything around us and partly because our bodies are becoming less dense, lighter and more etheric. It is as if we have been driving around in a family bus which can cope with a bit of blundering about and now we have got the keys to a souped-up, highly intricate sports car which responds to every nuance of treatment.

Losing our minds

Insomnia, forgetfulness and emotional vulnerability are three more very common symptoms as the planet lifts to another level. We go to bed tired and yet jolt awake at 2 or 3 a.m., as if hit by an electric shock, and then remain sleepless for the rest of the night. We go into a supermarket and forget what we came to buy, or catch a bus and find we have left the money to pay the fare at home.

In the last five years I have had problems when introducing my best friends to relative strangers. I remember the names of the strangers and forget the names of my best friends. As I stutter, stammer and blush, before mumbling, 'I can't remember your name,' everyone laughs, thinking I am being funny. I began to think I was suffering from premature senility or Alzheimer's disease and it was a great relief to realise that, even if I was, I was not alone.

Emotional vulnerability can affect us in various ways, from tears rolling down our cheeks while listening to music or watching television, to reacting in old ways to fears or situations we think we have overcome. Maybe our father or mother left home during our teens. We are jealous, insecure and enraged. We go out into the world, make a life for ourselves and get over the trauma when suddenly our husband, wife, or children, behave in a similar way and all the old fear, anger and insecurity come to the surface again, as if the 'rusty residue' from the past needs to be cleared.

Learning from our mistakes

The replay of old events, or difficult to deal with new ones, is happening in order to clear the emotional or astral body. As I mentioned earlier this body contains the imprint of everything that has happened to us, good, bad or indifferent. If we repress or deny the 'bad' or what may have been painful, it continues to affect us and will magnetise to us situations that draw the very feelings we have tried to repress to the surface. Many of us swallow our feelings – in fact lots of women gain weight around the abdomen and hips through doing just that. We 'put a good face on it', smile – sometimes through gritted teeth – and pretend things are OK when they are not. This can not only result in physical illness but also a form of false pride which, like a glass wall, separates us from both our inner being and others.

Old emotions are triggers to past experience and if we do not deal with them once and for all we go around and around in endless circles. Only after we have dealt with them properly can we be fully and creatively conscious and we must be that in order to participate in the changes unfolding around us. Life is now making very clear to all of us what has been hidden. It is like switching on a very bright light which shows up stains and cobwebs we never noticed before. In a similar way the violence erupting around the world does not necessarily mean things are getting worse but rather that they are becoming more visible. It is not very comfortable, so no wonder we feel vulnerable.

While some of us bury our emotions, others get as much sensation out of them as they can. Both are equally unhealthy. In the course of my work I have seen lots of people addicted to emotional sensationalism – or rather addicted to the rush of adrenalin that comes from fear, anger, hate, jealousy and so on. Even people who are constantly late frequently get an unconscious kick out of the panic to make haste. It is similar to the gambler who loses more than he wins because the adrenalin rush is greater when losing than winning. Like an addict dependent on heroin or cocaine he becomes addicted to adrenalin.

Sensationalism allows people who are stuck in their minds to get in touch with emotions they cannot contact in any other way. The thrill of being shocked by a film or play triggers a similar reaction. However, just like children who get a thrill out of being chased, or scream while playing hide and seek, we must grow out of it in order to discover real feelings.

Only then can we be clear to open up to the truth of our own lives and get in touch with our real selves, instead of being stuck in a past which we need to outgrow.

4

FOLLOWING
OUR OWN TRUTHS

Spiritual growth out of personal trauma

Shattering any illusions we have about ourselves, facing and living our own truth, is very much what the last decade of the century is about. Whether this happens through old emotions coming to the fore, or a catastrophe, it is a crucifixion of the ego. Like the crucifixion two thousand years ago it leads to transformation, pushes us to look at life from the Crown Chakra which, symbolised by the Crown of Thorns, ultimately gives a sense of equanimity and balance. It usually comes about through what we imagine is the very worst thing that could happen happening.

Obviously this is going to be different for each of us. One friend lost the use of her hands which she needed for her work as a physiotherapist; another was paralysed from the neck down after an accident. A writer with many books to his name could no longer get them published. Proud, forty-year-old parents, who had tried for years to have a child, produced a baby who was so deformed the doctors said he would never walk, talk or live a normal life.

For others this crucifixion may come through loss of

wealth, work or a child. No matter how it comes we are inevitably changed afterwards. These situations pierce the persona, the shell formed by the roles we play, the structure we put around ourselves, that encloses our understanding, compassion and humanity.

When something catastrophic happens, if we can acknowledge it and then get on with life, instead of bemoaning fate or blaming God, we rob the situation of its power over us. People who blame God, or anyone else, will always be victims. They allow what has happened and other people to dictate how they feel and what they do next.

If we could look at some of the things that happen as if they were dreams and say, 'Why? What is the message here for me? How am I meant to learn? How am I meant to change? How else could I have learned the same lesson? What is the difference in me now compared to who I was, or what I was like before?' and 'No matter if I've lost my health, my job, my wife and my friends, no matter how little there seems left, I am going to use that little to the utmost of my ability,' life suddenly co-operates with us.

A friend of mine, on the verge of finishing a thesis which had taken him ten years to formulate, returned home and found his house burned to a pile of ash, including the thesis, which he was supposed to hand in the following week. He sat beside the remains of his house for half a day, reviewing his life. With or without interpretation a phase of his life was over. He finally drove away and forced himself to rewrite what he could remember of his thesis. Instead of wasting energy on the disaster he fed it into his future. From that moment on his life took off in a new direction.

One of my own personal challenges in this life has been to deal with insecurity. Sent to boarding school at six I felt afraid, abandoned and no longer part of a family. In my late teens and early twenties I developed what I thought was a certain stability. Suddenly all my possessions – furniture, clothes, money and passport – were stolen. Within the space of eighteen months this happened three times. The first time

I was so devastated I thought I would die. The second time I felt bad but knew I must pick myself up and get on with my life. The third time I shrugged my shoulders and almost laughed. I knew I was being taught that the only security worth having was an inner security not based on outer possessions.

Through these and other experiences, I thought I'd learned the lesson well. However when it all happened again recently I suddenly realised I was not as immune as I thought I was. Feeling violated and insecure I wept. When a friend told me to thank the people who had done this to me, and who therefore helped release me from attachment to material possessions, I wanted to smack her in the face, even though I knew what she said was true.

My sense of abandonment at six came up again through many friends and acquaintances gradually disappearing out of my life – either through death, moving to another place or simply drifting into other things. This shifting kaleidoscopic pattern of people coming together and moving apart is nowadays a common occurrence. It will increase in the future. It is as if invisible strings are pulling us together with people we either have to learn something from, do something with or are part of our soul family.

There is usually a feeling of instant recognition, a compatibility and 'knowing' of each other, even if, in this life, we have never met before. On some other plane we saw the script, even helped to write it, had a dress rehearsal and now the curtain is rising and the play is about to start.

An actor in a theatre moves on to the stage and plays his part to the best of his ability. If he carried with him thoughts of all the people in his life who are not on stage with him at this particular moment he would forget his lines. It is the same for us. If we can live in the moment, value whoever or whatever is in our life today and bless and release them when they go, we can participate fully in our part in the play and not get stuck in loneliness and self-pity.

Obviously this is not always easy to do but it is something

to aim towards and leaves us as 'masters' of the events of our lives, rather than victimised by them. Then even defeat caused by our own conscious sins and omissions can lead us to say, in the words of Ashleigh Brilliant, 'I've learned so much from my failures that I'm thinking of having some more.'

The influence of Pluto

This process, which kills off past behaviour patterns and strips us of our old identities and props, is partly due to the influence of Pluto. Pluto rules elimination and regeneration; reflects the power of knowing when to hold on and when to let go, symbolises descent into the underworld, the downward spiral of spirit into matter. Plutonian energy stimulates self-confrontation, stirs us to face our own shadow – the repressed, neurotic, traumatised or unlived part of ourselves. This confrontation breaks down, and can break through, the crystallisation of old fears and taboos – another way of describing the crucifixion of the ego.

After confrontation or descent, which puts the personality in crisis, comes rebirth. The personality in difficulty behaves like a drowning man who, at his strongest the moment before death, is likely to attack his saviour, or grasp at any straw, in order to save himself. That straw may be drugs, alcohol or holding on to past bad habits. We can be destroyed by keeping Pluto's energy in check or we can use it to go through transition and rebirth; we can own, misuse or deny our own power.

In the past two or three years I have seen many people descend into the underworld, not always voluntarily, to find an aspect of themselves that has shocked both them and others. For example a woman who had previously led a 'blameless', somewhat passive life, catering to the needs of everyone around her and ignoring her own, suddenly began secretly to shoplift, while at home she expressed herself in increasingly violent temper tantrums. Whatever we repress we feed energy to. Finally it erupts like a pressure-cooker exploding. This woman had learned in childhood from an alcoholic, and frequently enraged, father that losing your temper or being honest about needs and wants was something you just did not do. It was not 'nice', it caused problems.

Pluto now forces us to admit the truth about ourselves, acknowledge that we truly feel, and accept that we are the sum total of many parts, 'good' and 'bad'. Once we integrate them they no longer have hidden power over us.

It is partly Pluto's influence which has shattered the façade of the British Royal Family. Anything corrupt, criminal, phoney or false – such as the Maxwell Empire, the Vatican Bank and dealings by some Italian politicians with the Mafia – is likely to be under tremendous pressure. Some of the major scandals blazoned in newspaper headlines across the world for us all to see are simply archetypal reflections of what lie in our own unconscious. Instead of pointing a critical finger at some of these situations we need to examine what may be phoney or false in our own lives and do something about them.

The next twenty years will see the structure of many established institutions which are not based on absolute truth crumble and collapse. Some of them are already beginning to do so.

Synchronicity

1992 in particular, especially the months of April, May, June was a year in which we had our masks stripped off. Time, space, spirit and matter merged together. Synchronicity and instant manifestation became increasingly common.

Synchronicity, a term coined by Jung, implies 'clusters of significant events occurring together'. For example, I may think of something, switch on the radio and hear an announcer simultaneously saying the very words I am thinking, or I may think of a friend and a second later he or she telephones, or knocks on my door.

Instant manifestation is an aspect of synchronicity. Whatever you need in the moment appears. Sometimes these may seem like very small, trivial coincidences, but once you start acknowledging them, you will find yourself opening up to the magic in your life. Recently, for instance, while travelling, I discovered I had left my toothpaste behind. In a hotel bathroom, with no immediate means of replacing it, I began to clean my teeth with soap when I suddenly found a half-empty tube left by another guest. Buying a take-away Chinese meal I realised I had nothing to eat it with. Wishing for a spoon I suddenly found one in the grass under my feet. (Whether I used it or not is another matter! The point is the universe provided.)

Today synchronicity also means instant karma – karma is the law of cause and effect. I express impatience with a person and five minutes later receive the same treatment from someone else. I see, but do not tell, that the checkout girl in the supermarket has given me too much change. As I place my purchases in the car my bag is stolen. When time, space, spirit and matter merge it is a little like being in the still, clear centre of a cyclone where there is no time, no space. Every now and again we are spun out and everything stops – as if we were in a time warp between dimensions.

This is partly why we become increasingly forgetful and nothing makes sense! I do not know who I am, who you are, or what I am meant to be doing! I go upstairs to get my purse, a coat, or to clean the bath and stand mesmerised, wondering why I am standing at the top of the stairs. I write a list to make sure this does not happen again but when I need it the list disappears. So do most other things when I need them. The letter I not only wrote but stamped and addressed is not where I left it when I go to the post office. The keys I know I put in my coat pocket reappear – two days later – under my pillow. So called inanimate objects apparently stroll about day and night, changing positions so they are never where I think they are, only to return when I have long given up hope of ever finding them again. When I was a child my Irish grandmother said it was because of the gremlins. If so the gremlins are now teasing us all.

The conjunction of Uranus, Neptune and Capricorn

At this time Uranus and Neptune are coming together in Capricorn, which means that 1993 promises to be one of the most potent times in the awakening of mass consciousness and the history of human evolution. It is the seed point in the change of our beliefs and attitudes, and will lead into a crisis of values and a breakdown of the old systems. The consequences of this breakdown can be seen through the Middle East, South Africa, Bosnia, the former USSR, and Cambodia. The year 1993 introduces a new beginning where man is stripped of his illusions and starts to take control of what he knows.

The discovery of Uranus, the rule-breaker, heralded new ways of thinking, coincided with the American and French Revolutions and the beginning of the Industrial Revolution. Uranus inspires us to break away from mass-conditioning to search for individuality, a new world and enlightenment. Neptune, the mystical planet, governs dreams, fantasy, illusion, psychic phenomena, the astral plane and stimulates telepathy and channelling. The recognition of Neptune as a planet heralded the use of ether as an anaesthetic, hypnotism, magic lantern shows as a prelude to the fantasy of the cinema, romantic literature and art, and many other forms of escapism.

Uranus and Neptune in Capricorn signify an increase of earth and weather changes, as part of the process of cleansing as well as revolutionary changes in government and other organisations which will ultimately produce a more humanitarian attitude to all of life.

To deal with these changes we need to be fully awake and able to move beyond the limitations of our own consciousness. It is therefore also significant that, in addition to the conjunction of Uranus and Neptune in Capricorn, we are – at this time of writing, February 1993 – entering the Chinese year of the Cosmic Rooster. Just as a live rooster heralds the dawn of a new day, so do the energies of the Cosmic Rooster accelerate our awakening.

In numerology, the science of numbers, 1993 adds up to 22. Twenty-two is known as a Master number which brings added potential for self-mastery and the opportunity to realise our unlimited potential. Twenty-two adds up to four which is a number of mastering the laws of the Earth, of balancing mind, body, emotion and spirit, of bringing all things into order. The two numbers twenty-two and four symbolise the concept of Heaven on Earth, or the linking of cosmic consciousness to planet Earth. It is a blending of the mystical with the practical.

The conjunction of Neptune, Uranus and Capricorn continues to affect us into 1994 and 1995. This conjunction as it moves through the 1990s stimulates, on the one hand, the recognition of our need for co-operation, communication and community, while on the other reminds us of our differences. We shall have the choice between saying: 'These differences are so great that we cannot live together' or to turning ourselves upside down in trying to see things from another point of view. If we take fixed attitudes and refuse to unbend we could see a world at war. The choice will virtually be co-operation or obliteration. As W. H. Auden wrote, 'we must love one another or die'.

Planetary alignments into the twenty-first century

According to Roy Gillett, a well-known astrologer (whose address I include at the end of the book), the planetary alignments of the 1990s bring confrontation between the forces of ignorance and the forces of enlightenment. He says we have a lot of hard work to do, both individually and collectively: we must face and overcome our karmic lessons and become stable, centred and disciplined. He predicts an expansion of the green revolution between 1993 and 2001 which will help to save us from attitudes to life based on scarcity, to a realisation that we have available to us everything we need, if we utilise our resources correctly.

The late 1990s will push us to face one challenge after another until we recognise that the one true solution to all our problems is to deal with their causes rather than with their symptoms.

A group of astrologers in America, known as the 'Star Fire Group' have analysed the Book of Revelation according to the predicted movements of the planets. They say that, in the sequence of star events laid out between 1993 and 1997, 'If, through awakening insight and feeling for the truth, human beings can perceive and follow the one who gives life after death, then courage to redeem mankind and the Earth will be rekindled.'

The Star Fire Group also suggest that 1998 brings with it several significant star events. As Pluto moves towards Antares, the heart of the Scorpion, on 26 February 1998, a total eclipse of the sun is due to take place. A similar solar eclipse on the same date 19 years earlier in 1979 signalled the onset of Apocalyptic signs in the Heavens and on Earth. Its repetition will mark a critical period and turning point for humanity. Each human being will be confronted with a conscious decision: 'Do I follow the lamb or the beast?'

At the end of this century there will be a major configuration of planets, a configuration that takes place once in a lifetime or approximately every sixty years. The Star Fire Group traced this conjunction back in history to AD 34, when they say there was a similar conjunction at the time of St Paul's conversion. This brings to mind that humanity will face a similar opportunity for conversion, and that it is this that will herald in the golden age of the twenty-first century predicted by so many throughout the world.

In any case, the current and future combination of stars, planets, signs, symbols and portents promise that no matter what problems we may face now – personal or planetary –

we really will see a change of consciousness that reconnects us to our own divinity, our own perfection, and enables us to become a part of the universal brotherhood of enlightened humanity.

5

LEARNING FROM THE MYTHS AND PROPHECIES OF THE PAST

The lesson of Atlantis

It was my first visit to America. I arrived in New York after thirty-six hours of sleeping with my fellow passengers on the pavement outside the airline building, due to a strike by aircraft personnel. Tired, crumpled and unwashed I was nevertheless stunned by the throb of the city and the vast, red-orange, rising sun which, like a huge Christmas-tree bauble, seemed to dangle among the soaring skyscraper buildings.

I decided to go immediately to the Empire State Building where I felt I could communicate with and talk to the Angel of New York. (I believe that each home, city and country has its own guiding, angelic force and that by communicating with this presence – greeting it when you arrive, thanking it when you leave, the place you live in, or visit, reveals itself to you in a different way.) From the Empire State Building I went to the Statue of Liberty and then on to the Meditation Room on the ground floor of the United Nations.

Having aligned myself with what I believe are three key energy points in New York, I began to have extraordinary visions of tidal waves engulfing the city. I saw what appeared to be Atlantis in its latter days – a shimmering silver city where men like gods flew through the air, over and under the sea, across and through the earth. If this sounds far-fetched, think of modern aeroplanes, submarines, trains, buses and underground trains. The Atlanteans were a highly advanced civilisation who knew how to tap the energy of the universe; who understood how to harness the energy of the sun through giant and carefully placed crystals. They used the resulting rays for heat and light (just as we use electricity today); for communication – similar to our telephone, radio and television; the development of psychic powers such as telepathy and clairvoyance; the transport of heavy objects; the invention of atomic power as well as the rejuvenation of ailing or deformed bodies (not unlike modern laser treatment). Even organ transplants were common at this time.

All over the world stories of Atlantis abound. Many of them have been written about in books, much has come from psychics and clairvoyants sharing their visions, while others have been passed from generation to generation by word of mouth. One of the first books to mention Atlantis was Plato's *Timaeus*, written in the fifth century BC in which Plato describes a conversation between a number of Egyptian priests and Solon, an Athenian statesman. These priests talk about Atlantis as a great island known as Poseida which existed as a vast continent between what we now know as Eastern America and Western Europe. They said it had been a powerful kingdom but because of the wickedness of its inhabitants it was destroyed.

Both Atlantis and its predecessor, Lemuria – or Mu – were founded on the Law of One; the belief in, the worship and love of, one God. As the Lemurians and Atlanteans moved away from this into the worship of science, power and material possessions, their civilisations began to fall apart. War, poverty, hunger, sexual indulgence and perversion were widespread.

As I looked across New York from the Empire State Building I was completely unaware of Plato, Voltaire,

Montaigne, Buffon and Francis Bacon who have all written about Atlantis. I simply had a sense of the destruction of a so-called 'perfect-race' brought about by their refusal to recognise and acknowledge the power of God, of nature and each other. In that moment I felt that we of this century are all reborn Atlanteans. We are presented with similar circumstances, have the opportunity to choose between construction or destruction, the brotherhood of man or the domination by one race or group of another. Also like the Atlanteans, who were given many warnings, we know change is coming but we are not willing to do anything about it.

Much of Atlantean technology supposedly came from extraterrestrials or beings from outer space who, according to a number of psychics, freely visited the earth at this time. These space visitors helped design the giant crystals which, in the beginning, were a tremendous force for good. However finally, through their gross misuse, enormous explosions were set off, devastating the land, causing earthquakes and tidal waves which washed the Atlantean civilisation off the face of the Earth. Before these cataclysms took place, wise men and uncorrupt priests, taking their psychic and scientific knowledge with them, began to lead small groups of people away from Atlantis to settle in different parts of the world. There they established schools in which mathematics, astronomy, engineering, writing and worship of the law of One were taught.

Cayce's readings on Atlantis

According to the Cayce readings, the destruction of Lemuria and Atlantis took place in three different phases with many years in between. The final one was a cataclysm so great that the world's topography was changed in an instant. Cold countries became hot, hot countries froze in the twinkling of an eye. This instant change of climate brought death to thousands of people as well as to many of the enormous animals, such as dinosaurs, that roamed the earth at that time.

Edgar Cayce believed this destruction came during a time when the Earth shifted on its axis and that this would happen again before the end of this century. He also predicted the reappearance of parts of Atlantis in the form of islands rising out of the sea off the American coast. Many psychics have pinpointed the Bermuda Triangle as the area in which the giant crystal, whose powerful rays helped to cause this pole-shift, lies. This is also an area where hundreds of people have inexplicably disappeared without trace as if the crystal rays are still alive.

World myths

During the past twenty years I have travelled extensively in many countries, including Africa, Egypt, Australia, America and New Zealand. I have spoken to Maoris, Aboriginals, American Indians and African witch doctors. Their stories seem to coincide, overlap and corroborate each other. Stories about people who travelled to the far corners of the Earth and who became the foundation of the black, white, brown, yellow and red races. Information handed down by word of mouth has become the stuff of legend, myth and fantasy. It cannot surely be coincidence that so many cultures share the same myths. I believe they possibly originated in Atlantis.

It is not only indigenous people who share these memories. Paco Rabanne, the world famous designer, claimed in a recent *Evening Standard* interview, that he survived banishment from the Crystal Planet, witnessed the fall of Atlantis and was swept away in the flood. He described coming to Earth with sixty companions on a flying saucer to build a settlement that would eventually become Atlantis. He said that initially Atlantis was cold so they decided to use huge, energy-emitting crystals to change the weather and make it warmer. The crystals turned out to be more powerful than the scientists expected and caused the Earth to turn on its axis.

The Hopi prophecies

I wish I had known of Paco Rabanne's beliefs before I went to

America because for many months after my initial visit to New York, no matter where I went, I had images of Atlantis and walls of water rising around me and began to doubt my sanity. I had a sense of what it must have felt like to have been swallowed up by a great wave of water. Then I read an article by a Cherokee American Indian physicist who described a life of being one of the Star people and how these memories fit together with many tribal legends. He said:

> We lived in domed cities with translucent walls. We could fly, communicate with animals, transport our-selves instantly to other parts of the world. I remember our city as a golden colour – a place of great beauty and calm. I came with others from my planet to help Earth through its birth pains into an intergalactic community and oneness. We were members of the priestcraft in Ancient Egypt; alchemists in the Middle Ages; scientists and clergy in the modern world.

Like many other native Americans or American Indians, he believes that there has been a close interaction between humans and the Star People, even to the point of having children, and that our current problems are caused by separation from the stars. In fact, the word 'dis-aster' means 'separation from the stars'.

Inspired by his words, I decided to explore more American Indian myths and legends. I found that most of them tell of previous worlds in which humanity reached great heights of culture and creativity but failed to honour the Earth Mother on which they lived or to acknowledge the teachings of the Great Spirit.

In 1970, Hopi Chief Dan Katchongua said, 'The Hopis were survivors of another world that was destroyed by flood.' Rolling Thunder, a Cherokee medicine priest, also talked about ancient civilisations, pyramids, prophecies, UFOs, Atlantis and what people can do now to prepare for coming events.

According to Hopi mythology, the universe was created by TAIOWA, the infinite creative force. In the beginning, all were attuned to the infinite. However, they gradually lost this connection and forgot their origins. According to Hopi elders, people 'lost the use of the vibratory centre at the top of the head, and the soft spot that was the doorway between the body and the spirit began to harden'. TAIOWA decided that this was not permissible so, while saving some people who were taken to the centre of the Earth, he/she ordered the destruction of the world.

In this legend, the North and South Poles shifted, resulting in an Ice Age. Hopi myths talk of people travelling in flying machines, but when they began to use them for war, TAIOWA sent waves taller than mountains to sweep over the land. Those who were faithful to the ancient teachings of the Great White Spirit became 'the Chosen People' and were sealed into hollow tubes so they could float upon the water. This sounds very similar to the story of Noah's Ark.

The Hopi prophecies talk about the 'True White Brother' who will come as the day of purification approaches. He will bring with him sacred stone tablets, matching the ones given by the Great White Spirit after the last time of destruction. These tablets contain teachings, instructions and prophecies.

To enable the Hopi leaders to check when the return of the True White Brother is imminent, certain signs and events were predicted. One was that white men would bring wagons hooked to each other and pulled by something other than a horse. Trains fulfilled this prophecy. They were shown roads in the sky, cobwebs in the air and lines across the land. These prophecies were fulfilled, the Hopi say, by airline routes, vapour trails, highways, electricity and telephone wires.

They were told that a 'gourd of ashes' would cause great destruction and believe this was the atomic bomb. Yet another prediction was that two brothers would 'build a ladder' to the moon – the moon landing – and that one of the last signs would be when man put his house in the sky. This could be the Skylab Space Laboratory that fell. After that the time of great changes would be near. Prophecies for three major world events are inscribed on rock and a sacred gourd rattle used in Hopi ceremonies.

One is the swastika, the other the sun and the third the colour red. The swastika symbolised Germany in World War II; the sun Japan and World War II. The colour red has yet to manifest but the Hopi believe that when the third sign comes it will either be complete rebirth or total annihilation. The choice is ours and depends on our balancing ourselves, changing our consciousness and living in harmony with each other and the Earth.

So seriously did the wise men and leaders of the Hopi take these prophecies that when they saw them come to pass they decided they had a responsibility to share them with the world. In 1948 and 1973 they went to the United Nations but were rejected. In 1976, in Canada, at a UN sponsored conference, they were finally allowed to deliver their message. This message basically asks us to honour the Earth as a sacred, living being who loves us like a mother and who, also like a mother, gives us a big shake when we behave badly.

The native Americans feel they are keepers and protectors of the land – especially the American continent. However, each tribe or nation has a particular duty. For example, Hopi means 'peaceful people' – 'those who follow a peaceful path'. They never fought white men, continue in a traditional way, to live on the land, farming and grazing cattle – trying to blend *with* nature rather than conquer her.

The Cherokees' prophecies

The Cherokees, known as the Principal People, understood the power of sound and crystallography. Cherokee means 'people who speak a strange tongue'. They have kept a fire, which they say, like their ancestors, came from the stars. They think of all mankind as Star People who came to Earth from Sirius. This is also the belief of the Dogon tribe in N.W. Africa – see Robert Temple's *The Sirius Mystery*. Dhyani Ywahoo, a medicine woman and Cherokee princess, told me that she was taught by her grandfather that, even when her people were forced to hide in caves, this fire was carefully carried and tended.

The Cherokees were renowned for their ability to heal with crystals. They still revere their crystal skulls which were known to sing and speak. These skulls were supposed to hold prophetic information about life, programmed into them in the same way that we store memory in computers today.

Like the Hopis, Dhyani also spoke of the 'Pale One' or 'Keeper of Mysteries', who not only came when people forgot their spiritual duties in the past, but will come again to 'rekindle the sacred fire', or share the teachings that will help humanity develop. Ancient prophecies, previously kept secret in order to protect them, and handed down by word of mouth, ceremony and ritual, are now being revealed to help us prepare for this time.

The Mayan Calendar and the Harmonic Convergence

The Mayan Calendar, deciphered by Jose Arguelles, says that the 'tide went out' in 3113 BC and will not return until midnight on Christmas Eve AD 2011. The Mayan Calendar came to an end in 1987 but predicted the importance of the years between 1987 and 2012. In order to share this information world-wide, Jose Arguelles inaugurated the Harmonic Convergence in 1987. This was a global cele-bration where thousands of people gathered together to honour the end of the world as we have known it, the end of Mayan timekeeping, and to welcome the new era coming in.

This is also a wonderful thing to do at the end of one year and the beginning of the next. To thank the old year, no matter what it brought into our lives, to then bless and release it, frees us, leaves us empty and open to greet the new year and the new opportunities it will bring. When the Harmonic Convergence took place, I was in South Africa. We planted a tree both for peace and to acknowledge the seeding of a new consciousness, a new understanding, taking root. To know that all over the world, at that moment, thousands of other trees were being planted for the same purpose, gave us all a sense of planetary connection.

A time of awakening

The Mayan Calendar states categorically that 2011 will see the birth of a new consciousness in the world and return to a time of trust and innocence.

This is not unlike the current expectation of people who await the Second Coming, the return of Jesus, Buddha, or the Maitreya, the rebirth of the Christ, the days of Rapture, the return of the Eternals, or the Peacemaker or Star People, who will descend from starry constellations to save us.

Throughout history we have gazed at the heavens searching for signs of life. Although most indigenous tribes believe they came from the stars – the Australian Aboriginals trace themselves to a race from the Seven Sisters, the constellation known as the Pleiades (others call this the Seven Dancers) – until recently most of us have dismissed such ideas as ridiculous. Now, after books by such writers as Von Daniken and Velikovsky, dramatic sightings of UFOs and supposed messages from outer space, even scientists are willing to take a second look.

The Aboriginals say they are still in communication with their brothers in the sky – in fact they too are awaiting the arrival of a new Star brother or sister who will help reshape their world. Aside from numerous claims from space-contactees that, not only have they been befriended by extra-terrestrials, but have also had joy-rides in a variety of spacecraft – which sometimes led to physical examination and sexual contact – there are also a number of men and women who claim to be psychic channels of information, fed to them telepathically, from outer space. Others have had personal 'on-the-ground' meetings with space people. One well-known such meeting was between Arthur Henry Matthews, a friend of Nikola Tesla, the electrical genius, and two golden-haired, blue-eyed men who said they were from Venus. They had come to see what Matthews was doing with Tesla's unpatented inventions. When Matthews expressed disbelief they said, 'When you see our ship you will believe.'

The leader drew from memory a sketch of an anti-war machine which only Matthews and Tesla knew about. Finally convinced, Matthews went with them and climbed aboard their craft. He was amazed to discover it was controlled by mind-power. In most cases of extra-terrestrial contact the messages have been of great love, while pointing out that Earth must work out its own 'destiny' without interference. Since then, hundreds of meetings have been recorded, indicating a large number of extra-terrestrial races on or above the Earth who, without direct interference, are choosing to play a significant role in our evolution.

Whether from the Book of Revelation in the Bible, old memories of Atlantis, prophecies from both ancient and current times, spiritual guidance, extra-terrestrial intelligence or scientists and biologists – the message is the same: a Time of Awakening is upon us.

Newspapers are also getting into the act with headlines such as: 'Is it Armageddon and the Apocalypse or the Advent of New Consciousness?' 'Is Jesus going to descend in a cloud to judge the living and the dead or will we be rescued by extra-terrestrials?' Recently, even before *The Evening Standard* newspaper ran a small article that said, 'If, by the time you read this, earthquakes have devastated London, fire has destroyed Buckingham Palace and the Thames has started lapping around your ankles, do not be surprised', an American magazine said:

The Time has come. You are chosen to lift your eyes from darkness to light. You are blessed to see a new day on Planet Earth. Because your hearts have yearned to see Peace where war has reigned, to show mercy where cruelty has dominated and to know love where fear has frozen hearts, you are privileged to usher real healing into the world.'

No matter where we look or turn, we cannot escape the message to WAKE UP.

Part Two

WAYS TOWARDS INNER GUIDANCE

6

THE HEALING POWER
OF THOUGHT

Once awake, what do we do?

First we must recognise that we have cut ourselves off from God and nature, separated intellect from emotion, internal from external, mind from body and body from spirit. We are dismembered like a Shaman or medicine man who, when undergoing his training, suffers a rending apart of everything that constituted his physical, mental, emotional and spiritual reality. Unless he can heal himself, through a reintegration of all his parts, the Shaman fails his initiation. We, like the Shaman, are moving through an initiation in which, to heal ourselves, we must re-member, or reconnect to, all that we have been separated from. Unless we do this we remain powerless to help ourselves, each other or the world.

I am reminded of a children's story I saw on television in which a teacher, desperate to occupy the attention of a recalcitrant student, tore to shreds a map of the world. Thinking it an impossible task he gave it to the student to put together. Within a few minutes the boy was back, the task completed. Astounded, the teacher asked how he did it. The boy replied, 'I looked at the pieces of torn-up world and turned them over. On the other side I found a torn-up man.

When I put the man together, the world came together and was whole again.'

Change from within

When we are awake enough to recognise that to heal the planet we must first heal ourselves, the next step is to explore how to go about it. There are literally hundreds of techniques we can use to put ourselves together. In fact, this generation is replete with self-improvement courses. There are courses on how to love yourself, how to know yourself, how to love others, how to deal with emotions such as anger, fear and jealousy, how to communicate, how to develop ESP. This list is almost endless. However, many of them work along lines of behaviour modification, structuring new ways of how to act and not necessarily how to be. In other words they work from the outside in and not from the inside out, but we cannot change the outside without first changing the inside.

Meditation

Change from within demands getting in touch within, as most psychologists, therapists and religious instructors would agree. To live in harmony with the world around us we must live in harmony with our inner selves. Meditation is the key.

In Chapter 2 I said that meditation transformed my life. Before this, I was an accident-prone, self-conscious, apolo-gising-for-virtually-every-breath-I-took, victim. Initially, to learn how to meditate was, for me, very difficult. I read that it was imperative that I sit cross-legged, close my eyes and blank my mind. I did and not only got cramp but itched and twitched in places I never knew were there before.

My mind refused to go blank, and raced from thoughts of what I would eat for breakfast, lunch and supper to all the things I had left undone the previous week. I bought more books. One said contemplate, another said concentrate; some said close your eyes, while others said keep them open, stare at a blank wall, a candle, a flower, a pencil. I tried them all. In the beginning I got up at 6.30 a.m.; when this did not work I got up at 6 a.m., then 5 then 4 a.m., until I was spending three hours a day, before going to work, furiously trying to still my mind, concentrate, contemplate, while agonising pains racked my stiff and resistant body.

Finally, in desperation, wondering how on earth anyone could find inner peace through such torture, I decided to abandon all the techniques I had read about. I still got up at 4 a.m. but I stretched my legs out and leaned with my back against a wall. I breathed in to the count of four, held my breath to the count of four, and sighed the breath out to the count of four. This gave my mind something to do, although it often went off at a tangent. However, I persevered until I suddenly realised I was beginning to sleep better and, although what I did was not meditation, through conscious breathing, my body began to relax and co-operate with me, rather than fight against me.

Having established a rhythm of breathing, which became more or less automatic, I decided to focus on the top of my head, my forehead, eyes and so on, down through my body to my toes. Initially I could never get from my head to my toes without some distraction but I always went back to the beginning and started again. Gradually I began to control my mind and I found that by the time I reached my toes, my body was so relaxed it was almost as if it wasn't there. I then practised moving my awareness from my toes to the top of my head and found myself arriving in a space where my mind truly did seem to be blank, empty and open.

I felt incredible peace and love, a sense of merging with something far beyond my normal physical consciousness. My life began to change. I saw the events and circumstances of my life in a different way. Living from the inside out rather than the outside in enabled me to deal with my work, family, friends and problems without stress or undue emotional reaction.

Over the years, meditation became the foundation from

which I moved into the day. It was as necessary as food and put me in touch with a source of guidance, healing and help which completely changed my life. Much later, I discovered there are as many different ways to meditate as there are flowers in a garden. Also that I could have found a class in which to learn which would no doubt have been far less painful and time-consuming. However, I did learn for myself that there should not be any rigid rules.

The books I read at the beginning were written in such a way that to even think of not crossing your legs in a yoga-like position was almost a sin. I now believe that, although there are many simple guidelines which can be helpful, it is far more important to discover what works best for you and this requires experimentation. Meditation should also bring a dynamic energy into our lives which enables us to improve the quality of life – it should not be an escape or an opting out but rather an opting in.

Meditation is a conversation not only with our inner selves but also with the God in us, the highest in us. If you or I decide to have a chat and we have children around, it is more than likely they will interrupt with 'Mummy, Sally smacked me', 'Mummy, I want a drink of water.' If we had taken the trouble to occupy the children first, given them a glass of water and crayons or toys to play with, they would probably leave us in peace. When we try to meditate or go within, our minds and bodies behave exactly like two spoiled children who demand attention from us and, in various ways, distract us.

If we take care of them first they will tend to co-operate with us rather than resist. For the body this means taking a few minutes to stretch, breathe, tense, tighten and then relax, the muscles; to occupy the mind, use imagination to fill the body with light or colour, then visualise a garden, a meadow, a beach, a mountain, a lake or stream – or the colours of the rainbow. It does not matter whether this comes from the memory of an actual place, a picture or an image you make up as you go along. It does need to be a place that engenders feelings of joy and delight.

Also the more you can let your imagination play, the better. For example, if you imagine a garden, think of the breeze rustling the leaves of the trees, the sound of birds, or water trickling, bubbling, feel the sun on your face, the grass under your feet, smell the flowers, hug a tree, splash water on your face. The more you can stimulate your inner senses to come alive, the less distracted you will be by your outside environment.

You also begin to create a safe space, as well as a backdrop – rather like a stage set – against which your inner life can unfold. To take the trouble to do these things before any deep inner work or meditation will help whatever you do afterwards to work better. They are a preparation for meditation but not meditation itself.

Some people find it easier to play music in the background but I suggest that if you are a beginner you do not use music all the time because it fixes in your subconscious the idea, 'I can only do this with music.' Then, in the future, if you are sitting for hours on a plane, train or bus, or are away from home, your meditation may not work. From my own experience I also suggest that it is better to start with a minute or two of sitting quietly, and gradually extend it as the days go by, rather than force an hour which may be difficult.

A very simple attunement to one's inner self is to sit for a moment or two, eyes closed, and say: 'I am in communion with the essence of my being.' The two words – 'communion' and 'essence', have an effect on our consciousness similar to that of saying: 'Be still and know that I am God.' It commands instant respect. Every cell in the body responds. As you say it, breathe deeply. This exercise will strengthen you and lead you into deeper and more prolonged moments of stillness.

For me, meditation works best early in the morning or last thing at night – preferably both! I feel more comfortable taking time out to sit or kneel, although I also sometimes meditate in bed. However, many of my friends feel they are in a meditative state while working in the garden, washing dishes, painting a picture, listening to a favourite piece of music, watching a rising or setting sun or gazing at a beautiful view. And this may be so for you.

Ultimately everything we do should become a living meditation. If we can, at least once a day, by what ever means are available, take the time to become still, receptive, and align with our spiritual selves, we will find we are no longer at the mercy of outside circumstances. We will develop our inner strength, need less sleep, improve our health and the quality of life generally.

Western culture emphasises the use of left brain logic. Two and two makes four and anything I cannot see, feel, hear, taste and touch does not exist. We deny the value of the right brain's ability to imagine, intuit, listen, sense and feel. To take time deliberately to drop the chatter and logic of the left brain and move into the rich creativity of the right through meditation restores balance and harmony.

In the final chapter of this book I include a few examples of ways in which to use visualisation as a preparation for meditation as well as some visualisation exercises which, rather like dreams, can help us explore different facets of ourselves as well as our past, present and future. Remember that as long as these parts remain hidden and buried they have power over us. When we discover them, and let them speak to us and heal and help them they, too, like body and mind, begin to co-operate with us rather than unconsciously holding us back.

The power of thought

Another step in putting ourselves together is to understand the power of thought. Thought is the glue that holds the universe together – thoughts, which are made up from the beliefs we have about ourselves and life, create the reality in which we live. I learned this lesson in the following way. For years my family disapproved of what I did and thought I was mad to drop a regular job and salary in order to wander about the world doing the sort of work I do today. Each time I went home, for days beforehand I would imagine who was going to say what, and wish I did not feel obliged to put in an occasional appearance.

Every time exactly what I thought would happen, did – often leaving me enraged and upset. After many similar visits I suddenly realised I was creating what happened so the next time, before I went, I imagined saying to my mother, 'I know you do not understand what I do but instead of attacking me why don't you simply say, "I don't understand what you do but good luck anyway." '

I then imagined light washing through both of us. For the first time there was no criticism or questioning, she simply accepted me. It taught me how the power of our thoughts affect what happens to us as well as the value of inner communication.

Energy follows thought, so if I constantly worry about war, starvation and poverty – or even my son falling off a motor-bike – I am actually increasing the likelihood of their happening. If I think I have an ugly body and hate myself, chances are my body, which is highly responsive to mind-power, will reflect that. By contrast, if I think beautiful, loving and appreciative thoughts about my body as the vehicle for my experience on this planet, it is likely to be beautiful and healthy.

During the course of my practice as a healer I have been involved with lots of experiments in which we took a random selection of people off the street and put them in a room with a highly competent healer. We then wired both the healer and the patients to a brain scan monitor. Initially everyone's pattern was different. When the healer put her hands on the shoulders of each person and thought of them, that person's brain wave rhythm became identical to that of the healer. It happened without exception, to everyone in the room.

We then took another group, again picked at random off the street. This time we placed them individually in various houses and apartments in and around London. We again monitored their brain wave rhythms with that of the healer, who remained where she was. One by one, she was given the Christian names of the participants in the experiments and again in each case, as she thought of that person, their brainwave became identical with hers. Her energy following her thoughts caused something to happen.

In other experiments we used muscle-testing or kinesiology. We sat someone in front of a group, muscle-tested them as they were, sent them out of the room, and told the group to send either good or nasty thoughts (collectively good or collectively nasty). In every case, when the person came back into the room and was tested again, the 'good' thoughts, such as 'you are wonderful', strengthened the muscles, while 'bad' thoughts – 'you are horrible' – weakened them. (We always put them right later.)

The interesting thing here was that muscle-testing those sending out the bad thoughts showed they weakened themselves as well. I often use this test to illustrate to people who are full of self-pity what they are doing to their bodies. They often make immediate decisions to change.

Another type of experiment has involved groups of people flooding different cities with positive energy, love and healing, while monitoring the results with the aid of police and social services. In every case, there was a marked drop in burglaries, accidents and violence. If we want to help the planet we need to use our minds to send out thoughts of love, peace, abundance and health to everyone. This includes leaders, heads of state, kings, queens and presidents whose track record we may not approve.

If we can say 'the Divine in me acknowledges the Divine in you even if I do not like everything you do', we separate what someone does from who they are and can still act as catalysts for healing. Instead of demonstrating on the streets against nuclear bombs or starvation we need to bring peace into our own lives and families and try not to waste food. Do not feed energy into what is negative; starve it of its power and the world will be transformed. As Margaret Mead said: 'Never doubt that a small group of thoughtful, committed citizens can change the world; indeed, it is the only thing that ever does.'

Controlling our thoughts

Many of us believe we cannot control or change our thoughts. 'This is just the way I am, the result of how I was brought up and what has happened in my life.' A thought is only a belief about something. If we can change our beliefs we can change our thoughts and move beyond limiting behaviour patterns.

A tiny example might be that I have a next-door neighbour whom I avoid because I believe he is arrogant and difficult. Years later something happens that forces us to communicate. I suddenly realise he is not arrogant but shy and preoccupied with work. I change my belief about him.

Even people who believe they cannot change surely do not think in the same way at seventy-seven as they did at seventeen? Life experiences change us all, and at this time world events are pushing us to move almost beyond belief of any kind. This means we are free to respond, in the moment, to whatever comes into our lives – which is the true meaning of the word responsibility.

For example, even if I am convinced that only homeopathy works and I deny the value of allopathic medicine, it is quite probable that at some point in my life, I am going to need penicillin. If I refuse the benefits of penicillin I may prolong my illness – I am limiting myself. If, on the other hand I am open to the idea that, although I prefer homeopathy and alternative medicine, I may at some time need a blood transfusion, operation or some other form of medical treatment it frees me up. To live beyond belief simply means acknowledging that what works for us one day is not necessarily going to be the same tomorrow or next week. It means being flexible, adaptable and willing to change instantly.

Beliefs are all right as long as they provide a loose supportive structure, but when they become inflexible, judgemental and restrictive, it is time to drop them. If your life is full of tension, fear and unhappiness, look at what you are thinking. Peace Pilgrim, an extraordinary woman who inspired many people to work for peace from 1953 to 1981 and who walked thousands of miles across the United States preaching global understanding and the need for peace, said: 'The criterion by which you can judge whether the thoughts you are thinking and the things you are doing are right for you is – have they brought you inner peace?'

Remember, your mind and your attitudes are two things that you have absolute control over. Also remember that you can only think one thought at a time, so replace a negative thought with the memory of something that makes you happy. It does not matter what it is – your favourite food or television programme – simply switch into another mode.

Beliefs affect our emotional responses. We think they happen to us as the result of another person's actions or attitude. In fact, we can choose whether to react or not, providing we involve the power of our mind.

Most emotional reactions are the direct result of the beliefs we have about ourselves. For example I, feeling insecure, go to a party and my husband dances a little too long, for my liking, with another woman. I am jealous. I have various options. I can interrupt, make a scene or say I want to go home. I can dance with someone else, I can go to the bathroom and cry, or take the car and leave.

If I act while stewing with suppressed emotion I am (a) going to regret it and (b) probably make a fool of myself. Whatever I do is an attempt to get his attention and reassurance. Through emotional reaction, that does not examine the underlying cause or belief, in order to get love I make myself thoroughly disagreeable and unlovable. It is completely irrational. If I could recognise that, in this moment, I am feeling vulnerable because of my own lack of self-worth – and be honest with myself about it, without blaming my husband – 'you're doing this to me'; if I could accept responsibility, look at the underlying cause, which is the belief that I am less interesting and attractive than my husband's dancing partner, maybe I could handle it in a different way. Maybe I could, with a smile on my face, tap him on the shoulder and gently say, 'My turn now.'

No matter how much we think emotions happen to us there is a moment of decision, an opportunity to choose between one reaction and another. The reaction we usually subconsciously choose is the one that gets the most results from the person or situation we believe hurt us. Most negative emotions come from lack of belief in ourselves. If I feel good about who I am, the fact that my husband dances too long with someone else will probably amuse me. I am not dependent on his attention for how I feel about myself. I do not give my power away to outside influences or let them affect what I feel, do or say. Even if I do feel emotionally vulnerable, by engaging my mind I can change what was previously an automatic reflex response.

Confused beliefs affect all of us. Recently a friend told me how, at a time of great personal crisis, he went to see a counsellor to pour out his problems.

'As I spoke,' he said, 'her eyes became a little glazed, she made strange grimaces which she tried to hide by propping her face on her hands. I thought she was so bored by my revelations that she was trying to stop herself yawning. In my family, no one ever listened to me and I became angry that even when I paid someone to listen they still switched off. I decided to leave. As I pushed my chair back, the door opened and a woman popped her head into the room saying, "Nancy, I know you've just been to the dentist to have a tooth out and I wanted to check that you were OK."

'I suddenly realised that she was in agony and that I was projecting on to her all my childhood experience. If this other woman had not opened the door at that moment, I would probably never have gone to another counsellor again and simply carried on with the belief, "No one ever listens to me." It shocked me into recognising that I had draped this belief over anyone I had any deep personal contact with, which created a barrier that made it come true.'

Most of us project our beliefs on to everyone around us – especially our families. A mother came to see me concerned that her son, aged eight, would only eat Coco-Pops. I said 'Does it matter?' She was outraged and told me that children should eat healthy food – plenty of fruit, vegetables, meat, fish and eggs. I asked why. As if I was a moron, she spent the next two hours explaining why. I finally pointed out that her belief about what a good mother was – to feed a child a healthy diet – was so fixed she was unable to respond to why the child was behaving like this.

Her need was to be seen as a 'good mother' which made her oblivious to the child's needs. It was a power struggle and probably the only way he could assert himself or get her attention. She finally saw that good mothering was not merely dependent on the quality of food a child ate, and followed my suggestion to start eating Coco-Pops herself. After about ten days of them both eating Coco-Pops for every meal, the child got bored and began to eat normally. The mother realised that quality time together, companionship and fun, rather than the rigidity of unconscious rules coming out of duty and responsibility transformed both her and her son's life.

Setting up expectations

If we expect ourselves, our children, or anyone else, to behave in a certain way, we and they will. An illustration of this is an experiment conducted in 1966 to study the expectations of the experimenters. Scientists ran rats through a maze. Half the rats had portions of their brains surgically removed, the remaining half received identical incisions, but no brain tissue was removed. The experimenters were told that the purpose was to learn the effects of brain lesions on learning. Some of the scientists were told they had brain-damaged rats, but in fact did not. Others were told they had intact rats, but actually had brain-damaged ones.

The results were amazing. The rats which were thought by scientists to be brain-damaged, but were really totally intact, did not perform as well as rats thought to be normal. The brain-damaged rats who were thought by the scientists to be normal, performed better than the rats who were actually normal but *thought* to be brain-damaged.

It was clear from this study that the scientists' expectations influenced the outcome of the experiments. These tests are very similar to the ones I described earlier using kinesiology to determine the effect of our thoughts on another person.

Thoughts change perceptions

Another more recent experiment showed that our thinking affects not only what we see, but also *changes* what we see. In a quantum physics experiment, scientists disagreed over what matter was made of. Some said particles, some said waves of light. When experiments were conducted to find the correct answer, it was discovered that those who believed in particles saw particles and those who believed in waves saw waves.

Was there a right or wrong answer? No. Reality depends entirely on our point of view. They also saw that they could affect the movement of both the waves and the particles through the projection of their thoughts.

This is similar to the experiments Marcel Vogel made with liquid crystals. When he projected the thought of a particular shape into the liquid, it solidified into the shape of his thought.

The power to re-create ourselves

Physics, metaphysics, science and technology now agree that everything is subjective, interrelated and determined by how we choose to look at anything. In other words, science reinforces the metaphysical teachings that say we truly do create our own reality and that there is no such thing as inanimate matter. Everything, from a cloud to a tree to a rock to the chairs we sit on or the car we drive, is infinitely responsive to our thoughts. We are creators of our own universe, we *can* cause things to happen.

This means we must take responsibility for our thinking – move from judgement, which condemns, to discernment which is clear-seeing. We must open our hearts to life and recognise that we have the power to re-create ourselves, our lives, and, like the story at the beginning of this chapter, the world around us. We are literally child gods growing up to be what our Father is.

7

USING CRYSTALS FOR
BALANCE AND VITALITY

Thought and electricity

Quantum physics has turned our thinking upside down and
drastically altered our perception of reality so that a new
paradigm (for change) is emerging. We now know that
whatever we do, think, feel or imagine, influences the world
around us. We as observers are not separate from what we
observe; by merely looking at, or experiencing it, we change
it. We impregnate it with a part of our own consciousness, our
own energy.

Thought produces an electrical charge. Highly emotional
thoughts carry a greater electrical charge. The atmosphere
around us is also electrically charged. Electricity is tenacious
of equilibrium; because thought produces electricity, the force
field in which cells, atoms and molecules are created is
affected by thought, which means that the invisible structure
of our surrounding carries a record, or the memory, of these
thoughts.

This is why psychics can pick up or tune into events that
have taken place in a room or a house. They 'read' what the
owners or previous inhabitants have unconsciously written

into the molecular structure of the place, space and furniture. Psychometrists who can describe the history of old jewellery, paintings and *objets d'arts* do the same thing. They decipher or interpret the impression or indentation left by past owners.

Crystals

Quantum physics proves that matter is a whirling mass of movement – a dance of quarks, protons and neutrons, sometimes seen as dots, sometimes waves – which is responsive to many energies including human. For example a plant will respond well to a crystal placed near it, just as it will flinch if a live shrimp is dropped into boiling water in another room.

Crystals themselves, which mainly consist of silicon dioxide and water, are of a high vibrational frequency which bring up to their own vibratory level everything within a certain radius. Crystals emit energy which expands when positive patterns of thought oscillate around them. In other words if we believe in their power they work better than if we do not.

Crystals are very much part of the new or quantum age in which we now live. They consist of millions of individual structural units of atoms called unit cells which link together in a network or pattern called a lattice. The effect of heat and pressure on these atoms rearranges them causing crystallisation.

Quartz crystals react when squeezed or pressed. They produce a current of electricity called piezoelectricity, an oscillation, which is why crystals are used in clocks, watches, radios, television sets, computers and any other electronic device that demands high precision. If heat is applied to natural quartz the stability of the atomic structure is disturbed, causing the negative and positive energies at either end of the crystal to change. As the crystal attempts to regain stability, by re-arranging the atoms of its internal structure, it produces opposite charges at either pole, which is called pyroelectricity.

Marcel Vogel, a research scientist and one of the world's most renowned crystallographers, had such an affinity with crystals that he could produce a flame from a crystal just by stroking it with his fingers. The ancient Greeks used crystals to light the sacred flame of the Olympiad. Australian Aboriginals, New Guinea tribesmen and in fact most indigenous peoples, including the American Indians, consider crystals to be the brain cells of Mother Earth, star seeds left by the gods or other planets, which have the power to heal, guide and transmit information. Many of the Edgar Cayce readings suggested that to wear a crystal or stone would give strength, vitality and protection to the wearer.

Crystals and healing

For twenty-five years quartz crystals have played a vital role in my life. I used them, in conjunction with prayers, meditation, visualisation and affirmation, to heal myself after an accident in which my face and head were smashed. The results were so successful I began to include, and still do, crystal work in my healing practice.

Crystals are not a magic cure-all, not a substitute for orthodox medicine. They can help kick-start the body – a little like recharging a car battery – to balance itself to a point of optimum health and efficiency. Crystals are transformers of energy and balance everything with which they come in contact.

During many experiments with doctors, both allopathic and alternative, we found that crystals accelerated healing and reduced pain. This included broken bones, post-operative scarring and skin problems as well as emotional stress. During one experiment we took people, one by one, off the street and measured their electro-magnetic or auric field. We then gave them a glass of ordinary water to drink. Nothing happened. As soon as we gave them crystal-charged water – water in which a quartz crystal has soaked for a minimum of

20 minutes and preferably longer – this field expanded to 15 feet around the body. The initial test was with 300 people and in every case the result was the same.

We may say, 'So what – who cares about the size of an aura – especially when to most people it is invisible.'

However the aura, almost like a bubble that enfolds us, is our very own private and protective space. It is an electrical field made up of a number of subtle or invisible bodies which swirl and move, shrink when we feel depressed, expand when we are happy.

Illness, mental upset, emotional distress, drug and alcohol abuse, as well as accidents and non-resolved problems – from this and other lives – show up in these subtle bodies before they manifest as symptoms of disease in the physical body. In fact seeing auras can even help diagnose learning difficulties in young children.

It therefore makes good sense to clear the aura of imbalance – which shows up like a shadowy blob or discoloration – as an automatic part of both general healing and preventative medicine. Crystal energy breaks up and disperses disturbance in the subtle bodies, helps to bring them into harmony and balance so that the auric field is cleared and recharged. This can be done by wearing a crystal, placing one on or near the body, drinking crystallised water or following some of the techniques I describe in my book *The Power of Gems and Crystals*.

Since writing this book hundreds of people have contacted me describing the results of their own crystal work. Sally, a woman in her late forties was in hospital for tests before undergoing major surgery. After urine tests the doctors said to her, 'There must be some mistake. We will have to do it again. Your urine tested as pure as a mountain stream.'

Every day for seven days, to the increasing disbelief of both doctors and nurses, Sally produced urine as pure as a mountain stream. Initially embarrassed, she finally confessed to drinking crystallised water. Incidentally this works best if the crystal, which should be natural quartz and not man-made, lead crystal, is left in a glass, a jug or a bottle overnight. In fact the water can be topped up as it is used and the crystal left permanently in place.

Clifford Jones, also a crystal-water addict, was confronted on his doorstep by a man selling water purifiers. They proceeded to the kitchen, where Clifford watched the salesman's demonstration and saw that there was indeed greater clarity in the purified water than the water from the tap. He then remembered the water jug in which he kept a crystal and asked the salesman to compare this water with the machine purified water. To the salesman's amazement — and I think Clifford's too — the crystallised water tested, and tasted, better than the water purified through the machine.

Frances, who attended some of my crystal workshops, fell downstairs and hurt her back. She remembered hearing me speak about crystals being used to reduce pain and so, while waiting for the doctor, held her favourite crystal against her lower back. Within ten minutes she felt the pain ease. Since then she has used crystals many times on both herself and others. For Frances crystals work best when placed on the area of pain and left for twenty to thirty minutes. (For best results, this should be done 2–3 times a day.)

Tom, a chain-smoker for fifty years, told me that he reluctantly accompanied his wife to a crystal shop and, while there, picked up a piece of amethyst, put it in his pocket and promptly forgot all about it. Two hours later he suddenly realised that since leaving the shop he had not smoked one cigarette, nor did he have any desire to do so. Wondering how this was possible he put his hand in his pocket and found the amethyst. Having previously mocked his wife for her interest in semi-precious gems he now decided that the amethyst calmed him to such an extent he no longer needed cigarettes. Overnight he stopped smoking. (He also went back to the shop to pay for the amethyst he had inadvertently taken and bought a number of other stones too!)

Jenny found that blue lace agate helped her sleep better while rose quartz held against her stomach after a miscarriage soothed feelings of distress and vulnerability. (Rose quartz is wonderful for any kind of love problem, including lack of self-love.) David, a doctor, put quartz clusters in his surgery and waiting-room and found his patients responded more quickly to his treatment than before.

Many healers use crystals, gems and minerals to balance and clear the chakras, the energy points in the body. Adolescents addicted to drugs and alcohol, when taught to see auras and treat them with crystal therapy, very quickly drop their addiction. Jane and Harry, both vets, began to use crystals on animals and found that they too, like plants, food, humans and even machinery, responded well.

Among the many other ways crystals can help us is through counteracting LVF, or low frequency vibration, caused by fluorescent lighting, television, radio, microwave ovens and similar electrical equipment. LVF used to be a method of protecting food stored in warehouses from rats and mice, until it was discovered that it made the staff emotionally unstable and depressed.

Today our bodies are constantly bombarded with all sorts of stresses, from insecticide sprayed on our food and the synthetic fabrics we use, to the polluted atmosphere, noise and even one another. Crystal energy neutralises these stresses by altering their atomic, molecular structure, the atmosphere around them as well as our attitude to them. Crystals played a part in the technology that sent rockets to the moon. In the same way they expand and energise us, activate our abilities not only to cope but to reach for the stars. They clarify what we need to see and stimulate us to deal with the results, even when we do not want to.

Aside from improved health and a general sense of well-being their effectiveness can be tested with kinesiology, biofeedback and Kirlian photography, a form of photograph invented by a Russian, Peter Kirlian, which registers the electro-magnetic field surrounding people, plants, animals and stones.

The power to heal is the power to control and move energy,

whether it be from one part of the body to another or from one person to another person. Crystals amplify and transmit this energy. The principle is similar to using a microphone which brings the voice into sharp focus, amplifies and transmits it in a way not possible for the human voice on its own.

For complete healing on every level we need to remember that illness exists first in the non-physical realm of mind, feeling and even spirit. This means it is essential to examine the whole person, treat the cause and not just the symptom. Quantum healing is holistic healing in which crystals are an invaluable part because of their capacity to affect every level of matter or vibration as well as every aspect of a personality, whether mental, physical, emotional or spiritual.

Choosing crystals

Having shared many simple methods of crystal healing in my crystal book I do not want to duplicate them here. For those who are not familiar with crystal therapy I want to stress that the crystals I refer to are naturally grown, quartz and not man-made which, however pretty, do not have the same power to balance or transmit energy. Neither do polished nor cut crystals have the same properties as those left uncut. It is as if their energy field is smoothed out and less active. However for people who need to be calmed down, rather than stimulated, polished stones are beautiful to hold and relax with.

A simple rule of thumb when choosing gems and crystals is to remember that the more opaque or solid in colour and texture, the greater its ability to absorb trauma and induce peace. By contrast, the more clear and sparkling the gem the more stimulating and energising its effect.

For example, *Herkimer diamonds* – tiny, double-terminated quartz crystals that look like diamonds and are only found in Herkimer County, New York State – are wonderful to carry with us when we feel depressed. They sparkle and glow, give us an extra boost of energy and help to clear emotional blocks. Anyone affected by criticism and what they fear or imagine others think about them will benefit from clear quartz, which generates and activates energy and repels negativity.

By contrast Malachite, Lapis Lazuli, Sodalite, Jade, green Aventurine, Sugalite (sometimes called Luvalite) are all opaque stones which sooth, calm and balance. Although each gem has its own particular qualities they all help to bring us to a point of inner peace.

Green stones such as Malachite, Aventurine, Jade and Emerald are especially useful for balancing the heart chakra, particularly if we need to develop unconditional love and peaceful relationships with ourselves and others. Green is known as the fulcrum colour, meaning it is the midpoint between the 'hot' or earthy colours of red, orange and yellow, and the 'cool' colours of blue, indigo and violet. It is therefore a colour generally associated with healing, and can be used to balance any form of stress, whether physical, mental or emotional.

Sodalite, which is a deep, almost navy blue stone, and Sugalite, a pinky violet stone, are both excellent for increasing spiritual awareness and developing our third eye or inner vision. *Blue* stones such as Lapis Lazuli, Sapphire, Blue Lace Agate, Blue Calcite, Celestite, as well as Turquoise and Aquamarine which, though not an exact blue, belong to the blue family, are connected to the throat chakra and can help us to release any fear we may have to speak out and live our own truth without apology or explanation. In other words blue stones release constriction in the throat and help us to express our thoughts, feelings and creativity freely and without inhibition.

The stones that can most help us to face the challenges of the 1990s and overcome some of the symptoms I mentioned in Chapter 3 are, firstly, *quartz crystals*, because they awaken us to higher levels of awareness and shatter, or break open, fixed patterns of behaviour, crystallized thoughts and attitudes.

Smoky quartz, which can vary in colour from black to shades of grey, can help us deal with the effects of Pluto who pushes us into the underworld. Smoky quartz helps us to face everything we may have repressed or denied, consciously and unconsciously. It triggers us to find and heal our shadow and as we do this the smoky quartz often becomes clear.

Rutilated quartz, which is a crystal with tiny threads of silver or gold running through it, is sometimes known as the stone of communication; its threads resemble telephone wires that connect us to places and people anywhere in the world. Rutilated quartz helps to focus and direct the mind, and contains within it the power to link us to past and future, as well as to friends and family, no matter where they may be.

Watermelon Tourmaline, tri-coloured Fluorite and Sugalite (or Luvalite) are also very important stones for the last decade of this century. *Watermelon Tourmaline* – which is pink inside and dark green outside – illustrates two different energies or vibrations blended harmoniously together, one contained within the other, and yet unique and individual at the same time. Watermelon Tourmaline is the ideal gem for male/female relationships – not for parent/child or co-worker relationships. They stimulate empathy, communication, companionship, and generate feelings of support and understanding that are sometimes quite uncanny. Watermelon Tourmaline can also be used when someone is dying. The pink centre contained within the green symbolises the tunnel of death, and can bring a peaceful acceptance that the time has come to float through it.

Tri-coloured Fluorite, which combines purple, white and green, symbolises the blend of will, wisdom and love, as well as body, mind and spirit. It can be opaque or translucent and is very much a gem for the twenty-first century, as it helps us to bring down into material reality ideas of the spirit. It is also good for teeth and bones.

The conjunction of Uranus and Neptune in Capricorn is helping us to move beyond only trusting and using mainly left-brain logic, while we deny the value of right-brain intuition and imagination. *Sugalite* clears away the barriers between logic and intuition, stimulates creativity and helps us to make quantum leap mental shifts that open us to other dimensions. It can also, like a Record Keeper, a quartz crystal with a triangle engraved on one of its facets, activate our memory of other lives.

The first time I used Sugalite I was totally unaware of its almost magical properties. I held a tiny piece of it against my forehead. Every chakra responded and aligned itself with the others. It was as if an army sergeant had caught me slouching and told me to brace up. At the same time I felt as though my brain had been tied up with Sellotape which was now being ripped off. I remembered the Barbra Streisand film *On a Clear Day You Can See Forever* and felt a surge of excitement that, in that moment, I could do the same.

Later a disbelieving friend took the same piece of Sugalite to her car and lay back with it pressed firmly to her third eye, or centre of the forehead, brow chakra. She was literally zapped into the memory of another life which so shook her that she returned the stone to me in shaking hands. However, it also clarified why she was experiencing certain problems in her life at that time and enabled her to deal with them in a different way.

Pink Kunzite, just like Rose Quartz, can help us develop self-love, self-acceptance, and therefore unconditional love for others.

Self-healed crystals – crystals which after removal from the earth grow another point or layers of little triangles which form a glittering, translucent pattern as opposed to the rough break formed by the crystal broken from its source, are especially powerful for the 1990s. They have learned how to heal themselves, and can help us to do the same.

Some of the crystals I have had for ten years or more have recently mended themselves in a way that is for me miraculous. This is one of the reasons why I do not believe in clamping a crystal at one end with silver or gold in order to hang it on a chain. This stifles its growth and blocks its opportunity for change. Self-healed crystals can help us make the best of every event of our lives, no matter how devastating, and bring them to a point of completion and harmony.

Another gem for the future is the crystal known as the *Elestial*. Elestials align with angelic spheres and combine the elements of fire, water, earth and air. They are often smoky grey with a configuration of geometric patterns and double-terminated crystals contained within a cluster. They are very comfortable to hold in the hand, can activate the crown chakra, stabilise mental confusion and help us with our true essence or soul self.

When choosing crystals for the first time trust your feeling and intuition rather than logic or what someone else thinks. An Aboriginal tribal elder told me once that when a crystal comes unexpectedly or spontaneously into our lives it is a gift from the universe, has grown itself especially for us and should be treated with extra care and respect. However whether we buy, find or receive crystals as presents, they are all very special gifts from the universe. Do not, therefore, get over anxious, fussed or confused when choosing one, the correct crystal for each of us will always turn up.

Experimenting with crystals

To discover how best they work, experiment. When I started using crystals I worked from intuition, trial and error. It was not until much later that I discovered scientific facts and explanations for what I sensed. Despite how much we learn about a crystal's geological make-up, and its ability to oscillate at different frequencies in clocks, watches, radios and computers, there is still a mystical X-Factor that even scientists have not been able to decipher. An example of this is the way in which crystals will disappear and reappear sometimes weeks later in another room, even another house or country. We should not feel sad about this but rather love and release them, knowing that they have moved into another dimension, a higher frequency, in exactly the same way that we move into another dimension at the time of our death, or release from our physical body. Many of my own crystals have developed *rainbows*, which are brilliantly coloured when I am well and become pale when I am sick. Others have grown new, small crystals, almost like a plant sprouting buds.

Rainbows reflect the link between Heaven and Earth; they are a sign of angelic protection and love, a blessing from God. Often the colour prisms which form the rainbows in crystals are there as the result of a knock or a flaw. Because of this they help us to transform our own flaws and knocks into beauty and understanding. Rainbow crystals can help to bridge communication gaps and problems with others with humour, joy and laughter. They are an antidote to depression and taking life too seriously. If we feel disillusioned by life and carry a rainbow crystal in a purse or pocket we shall soon feel better.

One of my initial trial-and-error experiments was to sleep with crystals under my pillow. I found that sometimes this energy helped me to sleep, at other times it kept me awake so that I had to move them to the floor of another room. I also discovered that crystals stimulate both dreaming and the ability to remember dreams.

The re-emergence of crystals

Many years ago during a ceremony of dedication in which a giant crystal played a major part, those of us present were told that we had all been involved in the misuse of crystal power in the past. As a result the energy and power were withdrawn. Now, hundreds of years later, this power was to be reactivated. We, along with the rest of humanity, had the opportunity to put right what we had previously done wrong. Since this time an awakening interest in crystals has occurred worldwide. About five years ago BBC Television produced a programme in which it was said that in the future crystal energy would be used in the same way as we use electricity today. I did not see the programme myself, but was told of it by a man who wrote to me saying: 'I heard you speak about crystals fifteen years ago and did not believe a word you said. I now believe it because how can the BBC be wrong?'

Crystals can help us to align with the changes now taking place so that we expand our consciousness and fulfil our greatest potential. Jung said: 'We should not pretend to understand the world only by intellect; we apprehend it just as much by feeling.' Crystals can help us to feel, open our heart to love, restore physical balance, uplift our spirits and bridge the gap between the visible and invisible. They are a vital aid to our evolution into the future and to promote our optimum health now.

8

DREAMS AS KEYS TO EMPOWERMENT

Dreams and crystals in history

Throughout history dreams, whether from the Bible, poets, authors, mystics and scientists or psychologists, have been used as a source of creative inspiration and knowledge not normally available to the waking mind. In the same way stones too have played a part in our evolution. Mohammed spoke and listened to stones, Moses received the Ten Commandments on stone, Peter was told by Jesus that he was the rock on which the Christian church would be built.

Early scientists such as Nicolaus Steno, a seventeenth-century geologist, and Abbé Haüy, Professor of Numerology at the Museum of National History in Paris in 1784 – who studied stones in the form of crystals – believed they had discovered an aspect of the mind of God, a sense of the underlying order of the universe. They saw the mineral kingdom as a point of communion between man and God, and crystals as the most evolved stone because they reflected more light and were therefore a God-given force to protect against evil.

The function and purpose of dreams

Dreams, though not necessarily a protection against evil, are also a means of communion between man and God. Quantum physics and thinking means to go beyond what was previously considered normal. Newtonian physics assumed that the basic elements of reality were like tiny bricks, absolutely fixed in number. Quantum physics recognises that its basic elements of neutrons, protons and quarks change all the time. It is an expansion of awareness, a quantum leap into another reality. Dreams and crystals, because they blend the visible and the invisible, bridge both physical and non-physical worlds and can help us make this leap.

Dreams mediate between left and right hemispheres of the brain, logic and intuition, male and female, active and passive, positive and negative. They are a source of power, knowledge, creativity and health. The Talmud says that to ignore a dream is like receiving a letter and leaving it unopened.

When we sleep and dream we are in touch with a wiser, more detached part of ourselves that gives an honest assessment of how we really think and feel as opposed to how we pretend we think and feel in waking life. For example Jeff dreamed of Dolly Parton picking his pockets. When asked what Dolly Parton meant to him he replied, 'a female who uses plastic surgery to retain her sexy image'. When asked who in his life reminded him of Dolly Parton he thought of his girlfriend, who continually borrowed his (plastic) credit-cards to buy clothes and pay bills, to improve her appearance, which he considered to be her responsibility rather than his. His dreams made him consciously aware of how upset and frustrated he felt and finally led him to talk to her about it.

To pay attention to dreams is similar to looking at life from a helicopter, instead of driving a car along a road on the ground, where our vision is limited to what is immediately around us. From a helicopter we can see what is going on from a totally different and wider perspective. We can also see what lies behind and what is emerging ahead, we can see the interconnections, the interweaving pattern of events and our place in them. A dream is a psychic reading, our own personal Akashic record. The Akasha is described by some religions as the memory and mind of God. It is the record of everything that has ever happened, written, according to Edgar Cayce, on the invisible 'skein of time and space' in the fabric of the universe.

Dreams allow us to play and experience many roles, and can often solve problems in creative ways that would not have occurred to us in waking life. Numerous dream discoveries have improved our quality of life, both scientifically and artistically. The German chemist, Kekulé, discovered the molecular structure of benzene through his dreams and later, when reporting his findings at a conference, said: 'Let us learn to dream, gentlemen, and then we may find the truth.' Both Harvard Business School and Stanford University have programmes in which business men and women are taught to use dreams to solve problems and bring in new ideas.

Dreams reflect and help us to explore – and even change – our innermost beliefs, face our fears, and create new options in our lives. They help us understand ourselves better so that we stop projecting on to others our faults, failures and weaknesses.

Many years ago Freud said that dreams were the Royal Road to the unconscious. Today most psychologists and dream therapists would say that dreams are the Royal Road to life itself and not just tools of diagnosis for the mentally ill. An illustration of this is the American Indian or Australian Aboriginal, who, if separated from his Dreamtime tradition, loses his sense of identity with his family, tribe and community.

Unlike indigenous people who have always valued dreams, omens, visions, hunches and telepathy, and used them as an aid to survival, most of us have learned to deny the value of our own inner wisdom. Instead of relying on our inner senses we switch on the radio or television, or pick up the telephone to obtain information about current events, people and the weather.

These instruments, which so fascinate us, are in reality only outer reflections of the inner abilities we all have. Instead of respecting them, most of us have let them atrophy. As a result we feel cut off from an innate part of ourselves, one another, the Earth and nature. It is not difficult to reawaken these abilities and dreams are one of the simplest, safest and most exciting ways in which to do so.

Working with dreams

1 Valuing dreams

The first step in working with dreams is to decide to value them. A dream is part of the psyche's balancing system and as such deserves our respect. Even people who swear they never dream, do so four to five times a night and would become psychotic if they did not. In fact the average person spends a third of his life asleep and six years of that dreaming – enough time to graduate as a surgeon, chemical engineer or scientist. What a waste of the brain's potential not to use it during this time.

2 Preparing for sleep

The second step is to prepare for sleep. Most of us fall into bed at the end of a long day only to toss and turn, trying to relax. We could sleep better and dream more productively if we did a little groundwork first. Dreaming takes place when our brain-wave rhythm moves from Alpha into Theta, both slower than Beta, the active, decision-making level we use when awake.

Deep breathing, tensing and relaxing our muscles, creative visualisation, listening to music or holding a crystal, all help to put us into Alpha very quickly, which means that we shall be much more relaxed when we get into bed. Creating a peaceful atmosphere in the room around us with flowers, herbs, incense, crystals or candles will also induce deeper sleep and dreams.

If we did no more than mentally honour the night, sleep and dreams, as we got into bed, already the quality of our sleep and dreaming would improve. However the more effort we put into pre-sleep rites, the more we impress our unconscious, subconscious and higher conscious selves that we are really serious about what we are doing.

Another vital part of sleep preparation is to leave the day behind. No matter what went on, nor what we or anyone else did or did not do, try not to carry the day into the night. We can mentally sum up the day, good, bad or indifferent, and breathe it into a crystal, let it flow out of our feet into the bath or a bowl of water, or into the air in a visionary balloon.

Best of all is to make a note of day-to-day events, especially those with the most emotional impact, the lessons we believe we are meant to learn from them, the people who make an impression on us (good and bad), recurring incidents and general insights. Dreams at night are usually a running commentary on our daily lives – while also reflecting past and future. To keep some sort of record or journal helps us to understand both our dreams and what is going on in our lives at the same time. Before turning out the light do not forget to write down: 'I want to dream and to remember my dream.' This programmes our dreaming selves to respond and can also be used as an affirmation before sleep.

3 Dream recall

The third step in dream work is to learn to recall and record our dreams. Dream recall is an acquired habit and not difficult if we are prepared to practise. Remember that we dream less if we are under a lot of emotional stress, or take pills, drugs or alcohol. Also many of us forget our dreams because we are woken by an alarm or children or by getting out of bed too quickly. Try and wake a few minutes earlier and immediately write down whatever you can recall of your dream.

Never go to bed without leaving pen and pad beside you. If you wake naturally during the night try to write down whatever you can recall of your dreams. You may initially find it easier to speak into a tape-recorder but even if you do, to write a dream down is more powerful. You are literally making the invisible visible – and it affects our consciousness in a different way.

If you wake up with a huge dream scenario that vanishes as you reach for your pad, relax back into the position you were in as you woke; breathe deeply and ask for the dream to come back. If nothing happens roll into a new position. If the dream does not return, simply describe the feelings, the colour of the dream, what you did yesterday, what you felt when you went to bed. It is essential to write something, rather than leave the page a blank. This not only emphasises to your dreaming self the importance you are giving to dreams but will often catalyse your remembering of them.

If the above suggestions do not work for you, you may find taking Niacin and B6 (the mental vitamins) for a short time helpful. A lack of these can also upset our emotional balance. A shortage of B6 makes it difficult to remember dreams. Another catalyst is to drink half a glass of water just before sleep. Affirm, 'I will wake up and I will remember my dreams.' Immediately upon waking, drink the other half and repeat the affirmation. This helps to fix the idea of dreaming in your mind, which like a computer, gives out what you put into it. These steps are simple and they work. However, if you have never paid attention to dreams before, you may have to practise to get results. The most important step is the decision to try and often that alone stimulates a dream.

When writing a dream down note the key symbols first, such as names, numbers, words, plus figures of speech. Often dreamers lose these by concentrating on recording the dream story. Also watch what comes up over the months ahead such as recurring dreams or symbols. Dream symbols disguise feelings. Dream interpretation means translating the picture back to the feeling. This is not difficult. By concentrating on symbols we can merge with them and then discover what they are and where they came from. To observe and contemplate outer life events can lead to similar discoveries that help us understand why our lives unfold in a certain way.

Experiencing and interpreting dreams

People in dreams, even if they appear as the milkman, or the boy or girl next door, should always be interpreted as aspects of oneself first, no matter what secondary meaning they might have. We should look at the quality in us which this person may represent, why is he/she in the dream, what is he or she doing, saying, feeling, and what is this telling us about ourselves? If we have never seen this character before is there anything about him or her that reminds us of someone in our waking lives? In fact, while writing dreams down we should constantly refer back to waking life – what does this feeling, setting, person, activity or symbol remind us of?

We must keep asking questions of ourselves until the answers pop up. It becomes easier and easier with practice. When we have recorded the dream, we should make an intuitive guess at what we feel the dream is saying, its overall meaning for us and our lives, rather than an intellectual interpretation.

Finally we should always decide on what action we are going to take to implement the dream's message. This is an aspect of dreamwork that is often left out. By actualising the dream, even if it is only to wear the colours in it, or contact the person we dreamt about, we draw an energy into our lives that can empower us to live with greater freedom and happiness.

Nightmares and recurring dreams

Never be afraid of what appears in a dream. There is nothing in the unconscious which is not already in life. Any fear or apprehension will often be exaggerated in the form of a monstrous apparition.

The best way of dealing with a nightmare is to get back into it as quickly as possible and face it. Imagine being back in the dream again. Confront the threat, point your finger at it, question it: 'Who are you? What are you? What part of me do you represent? What do you want me to know? – do? How can I help you? Heal you?'

Usually just to face the threat, rather than run away, transforms the energy embodied in the dream image. For example, a friend had recurring dreams in which her husband pushed her overboard into a deep and seemingly bottomless sea. The terror, as she sank deeper and deeper into the water, always woke her.

Guiding her back into the dream, suggesting that she stopped struggling and allow herself to float down into the depths to see, either what happened next, or what might be down there, cured her of her fear and stopped the dream recurring. She discovered life in the ocean depths, colourful gardens and a beautiful woman who sang as she handed the dreamer a silver platter of exotic fruit.

Suddenly her husband appeared beside her and they ate the fruit together. She realised that in her previous relationships with men she was so emotional that she drove them away. Now married, she was afraid to show the depth of her feelings in case the same thing happened. Her husband was an emotional man himself, and often unconsciously triggered situations that pushed her overboard, into her feelings.

By going back into her dream she saw now that there were treasures to be gained from letting herself feel deeply and that the depth of these feelings could be expressed (the woman singing) and shared with her husband. In exploring the rich, emotional life of her unconscious she freed a feared, repressed and unlived part of herself. Dreams and imagination can help us all find and heal split-off parts of our personality – often referred to by Jung as our shadow selves.

Nightmares and recurring dreams, which often take nightmare form, are emphatic demands for us to pay attention, a call from our inner to our outer selves to listen, an attempt to wake us from sleep to life. They usually reflect fear, frustration, resentment that our needs are not being met now or were not met in the past, or that something is wrong in our lives. Like all dreams, nightmares and recurring dreams try to point out what we feel and think unconsciously and subconsciously but they do it with an extra kick, which, at the same time, releases a lot of repressed emotional energy.

They often include dreams of being chased; running away and our feet will not move; crying for help and no one answers; taking an exam and our minds go blank; having to give a speech or talk and when we open our mouths no sound emerges, or our notes fly away; falling off a cliff, out of a window, down the stairs or into a black hole; searching in vain for a toilet; walking down the street and our clothes fall off, or we suddenly realise we did not have them on in the first place; our hair and teeth fall out or our faces shatter and disintegrate as we look in the mirror; losing handbags, wallets, money, tickets; missing trains, planes, buses or important appointments; forgetting where we live or where we parked the car. The list is endless and all these dreams are very common. They have an underlying anxiety to them – a fear that, 'I will not appear or perform as I am expected to.'

In all dreams we need to look at how comfortable we were. Did we feel vulnerable, threatened or quite happy when we lost our teeth, changed sex, or sat on the toilet in front of the Queen? During a live radio programme on dreams a young girl phoned in and described a recurring dream in which she saw her own face sporting a luxuriant beard and moustache. I asked her how she felt in the dream. She replied 'Proud. It was only when I woke that I felt concerned and upset.'

I asked her what a moustache and beard meant to her and she said, 'Power, masculinity.' By going through the dream again she realised she could reveal her masculine side with pride, that it was part of, and perfectly balanced with her femininity. If her entire face had been covered with hair it might have meant she was using male energy, the more assertive side of us, to disguise her femaleness. In fact lots of women do this in life, fearing that to be 'just a woman' is not enough.

Dreams of exposure

So common are dreams of either finding oneself in an unexpected, and usually public place, losing bits of clothing or having them torn off by someone else, that, based on research, an advertising campaign (about twenty years ago) created a promotional idea for women's bras in which the woman's blouse or dress fell away to reveal the bra underneath. The caption said, 'I dreamt I was at the opera ..., Madame Tussaud's ..., Kew Gardens ... or wherever ... in my XXX bra.' It proved to be one of the most successful advertising campaigns of all time, both men and women relating to it.

Dreams of being naked or semi-naked can symbolise a healthy willingness to 'let it all hang out', to expose freely and express all that we are, or a case of 'I'll show you' almost like a threat. Embarrassment at being naked may signify a fear of exposure, a need to cover up not merely the body but an aspect of one's life we consider shameful.

In dream research women who feel insecure often dream of being abandoned in an unknown area, while men dream of fighting and shooting, desperately trying to establish their identity. Dreams like this indicate a need for help – which usually the dreamer feels is not available. Radio and TV announcers, actors and actresses, frequently dream of either arriving late or forgetting their lines. Aside from indicating an insecurity about what they are doing it can also be a nudge to prepare better for a particular task. This type of dream is also common to ambitious people who feel they cannot quite keep up.

Reducing threats in dreams – and in life

Apart from exploring the dream's message if we can learn to send love, point a finger, a crystal, a colour, light, or whatever may be meaningful to us, towards the threat it always changes it, either into a smaller version of itself or something quite different. Children who are taught to do this in their dreams learn that in life, by always facing a problem, they can shrink it to a manageable size. We can all do the same.

Connecting to yourself through dreams

In fact children who are encouraged to share their dreams from the moment they can speak tend to become far more verbal, creative, emotionally expressive, and willing to discuss problems as they grow up than children who are not. Research also discovered that heart patients who were taught to use dreams as part of their after-care therapy, which include pre-sleep breathing and relaxation techniques, recovered 60 per cent better than those who decided it was irrelevant.

Pregnant women were also discovered to give birth more easily after using dream-therapy during pre-natal care. Teenagers, when introduced to dreams as part of their curriculum, not only absorbed information better and therefore learned more quickly, but also passed exams more easily. To pay attention, to listen to dreams means we connect to a wiser and more intelligent self than the one we usually know and use, as well as to an energy that empowers us to behave differently.

There are as many ways of working with dreams as dreams themselves. These include art, music, mime, dance, acting, drawing, painting, sculpture, gestalt, incubation, dialogue, re-entry as well as writing them down. Remember that the language of a dream is unique and individually tailored for each dreamer. Therefore the more we listen to a dream, immerse ourselves in it, meditate or ponder on it, the more likely it is that the meaning will reveal itself to us. Like learning another language the more we practise it the more proficient we become.

The significance of a dream

People who choose to interpret dreams from a dream dictionary tend to get stuck with the surface meaning, instead of understanding the emotion, or waking life event, that underlies the dream's message. Remember too that each part of a dream has meaning, sometimes more than one. A dream that says one thing today can reveal a completely different idea a few days later.

Dream interpretation should be simple, practical and help us to improve our everyday lives, as well as our understanding of ourselves and others. For me the guarantee of a dream's importance is the emotional impact within the dream and the electrifying burst of energy with which I wake up. Even without specific interpretation I believe that a dream has been understood and integrated when one's life changes as a result. Through dreams and dream incubation (to ask for help, healing or insight) we have available to us an intelligence that can answer any question we may have about life. This intelligence is sometimes called the Higher Self, the Soul, or Super Consciousness. Jung called it the collective unconscious and described it as a human being combining the characteristics of both sexes, transcending youth and age, birth and death and having at his command a human experience of one or two million years. Edgar Cayce referred to it as 'a river of thought, fed by the sum total of man's mental activity since his beginning.'

The last decade of this century is pushing us to move beyond automatic-pilot consciousness, to stop looking outside for the answers and instead to search within where the answers are to be found. Dreams – the Language of the Gods – are one of the most important keys to this wisdom.

9

HONOURING
THE EARTH

The ecological crisis

'The world is in one hell of a mess. I think one third of it is now so far and deeply destroyed that it is going to cost us mega-billions to put it back into working order.'

So said renowned scientist David Bellamy when speaking at the Australian Association for Environmental Education Conference in 1992. Among the many ecological problems he discussed were cars.

There are more cars in Los Angeles than in the whole of China, India, Pakistan, Bangladesh and Indonesia put together. If cars in Britain reached saturation point it would require roads, and their parking spaces, the equivalent of a motorway from London to Edinburgh 944 lanes wide.

He also spoke of the North Sea's acid rain:

The north east coasts of England and the coasts of Europe are now so bad that you can no longer eat the shellfish. The poisons are actually getting into the filter feeders. Not only do poisons go into the foods chain but more acid rain is generated.

(We need *some* acid rain, but too much, especially from over-entrophication of the sea, destroys trees, which in turn affects the soil, lakes and rivers.)

He had this to say about the Alps: 'One third of all the traffic in Europe squeezes through the Alpine passes, and the resultant pollution is a kind of creeping death that is killing off all the trees.'

'We've got about ten years in which to save the world. If we don't act now, then, within that period of time, many of the earth's species will be extinct,' says Helen Caldicott, MD, founding President of Physicians for Social Responsibility, and member of the 1986 Nobel Prize-winning International Physicians for Prevention of Nuclear War.

There are only ten thousand elephants left [she continues]. There used to be millions when I was a child. They have become endangered because we like to wear their tusks on our wrists and on our ears. Rain forests are being chopped down to create land to raise cheap beef to give us hamburgers which are no good for our health anyway. We did not evolve eating meat – we evolved eating grain. The amount of grain that is now used in America alone to feed cattle could feed all the starving people in the world. Meanwhile, two-thirds of the world's children are malnourished . . . The ozone layer is disappearing faster than was predicted. For each 1% decrease in ozone, there is a 6% increase in skin cancer. The dermatologists in Australia have seen a doubling of malignant melanoma in the last ten years.

Jeremy Rifkin, President of the Foundation for Economic Trends, and of the Greenhouse Crisis Foundation of Washington DC, when discussing the global environmental crisis, said:

Our generation faces the first true global environmental crisis in recorded history. While our ancestors experienced traumatic environmental threats, they were limited to specific geographic regions. Now, as we near the second millennium, a new environmental threat is emerging so enormous in scope that we find it difficult even to fathom. We have no equivalent past experience from which to mount an appropriate response.

David Bellamy ended up by saying: 'Perhaps this is the kick in the pants we've been waiting for. We've got to start caring for the land. If we don't care for the land the land won't care for us.'

How we can help

So, how do we cope, what do we do?

First, we need to focus on what is possible and changeable, rather than on what is impossible and immutable.

The word 'ecology' comes from the Greek word 'oikos', which means 'the household'. Ecological responsibility therefore begins at home. The Earth is dying from global warming, caused by over-use of cars, machinery, electricity and oil. We add to global warming by switching on unnecessary lights, using hair-dryers, air-conditioners, washing-machines and electric refrigeration, as well as plastic containers, spray air deodorants and air fresheners. Newspapers, magazines, packaging and toilet paper are products of trees being cut down without adequate replacement. Much of today's packaging is plastic, which, made from oil, produces almost indestructible toxic waste that no one really knows what to do with.

Maybe our first step is to look at how, individually, we can improve things in a practical way. We can stop blowing our noses on paper tissues, using our cars unnecessarily, and buying products prettily wrapped in five layers of packaging.

We could let our hair dry naturally, stop using sprays of any kind, recycle jars, bottles, egg-boxes, newspapers and magazines, use our bath-water for the garden, and stop letting the tap run when we brush our teeth. We should eat simple non-processed food. If we don't have the facilities to grow our own food we could buy direct from people who do.

Planting trees

We could also plant trees, which provide oxygen, and of course adequate oxygen is essential for healthy and stable human life. Richard St Barbe Baker, known as the Man of the Trees, and Hans Selye, MD, an expert in stress control, found in experiments on rats that lack of oxygen stimulated violence. A tree planted when a child is born, and dedicated to it, will monitor that child's growth. It will grow, break or bend and shape itself according to what the child experiences as it develops.

The Essene community, to which Joseph and Mary the parents of Jesus belonged, planted a tree for every year of a child's life until it reached maturity. These were probably fruit trees, and no doubt provided a means of support and stability. The Essenes encouraged their children to plant trees. Shouldn't we do the same?

Some years ago a fifteen-year-old schoolboy in Los Angeles decided that the city needed more trees. Near his home was a plot of land on which was an old, disused fire station. He thought that, with the aid of friends, he could fill it with trees and sell them. He approached the local authorities with his idea. They not only refused him permission, but also roared with laughter that a mere schoolboy should even think of anything so crazy. For six years this same boy persevered, contacting local councils, schools, businessmen, politicians, churches and other organisations.

Finally, when he was twenty-one years old, the authorities capitulated and said: 'OK. Do it!' Through this boy's idea, guts and determination a million trees were planted in Los Angeles. If one fifteen-year-old boy can instigate a programme that results in a million trees being planted in a city which desperately needs them why can't we all try to do something similar? Even if each of us does no better than plant one tree a year, the total improvement could be tremendous.

Trees, with their roots in the ground and their branches reaching up into the sky, blend heaven and earth, spirit and matter. In some ancient philosophies the tree was used to illustrate oneness with all of creation. It was a powerful spiritual symbol to study and emulate. Most of us feel completely renewed when we walk through woods and forests, especially the type of forest where the trees are so tall there is almost no light, and the sensation is similar to that of bathing in a cool green pool.

Communication with trees

Trees absorb and transmute our negativities, releasing us from them. Rocks and mountains do the same. Every tree has a spirit, an angel, and all we have to do to communicate with it is to hug it or to sit with our backs against its trunk. Like holding crystals, this is a simple and effective way of revitalising ourselves when we feel tired. If you do this, do not forget to give something back, in the sense of sharing yourself with the tree, and thanking it.

Many years ago, I was in a forest hugging a huge tree, whose trunk was so vast that even with both arms outstretched I could not anywhere near reach round it. After about thirty minutes the tree seemed to speak to me, and said that enormous healing energy was being poured into the Earth at this time, and that all we had to do was to open ourselves to it every day. We would then immediately catalyse healing in everything around us. We did not need to go around deliberately laying our hands on people or things, but rather, before getting out of bed in the morning, to mentally affirm: 'I offer myself as an instrument of healing for whoever and whatever comes into my life today.'

When we do this, we affect everything we touch, from the car we drive to the pavement we tread, and the desk we sit at. I have made a practice of doing this ever since, and feel that I benefit as much as or as more than anything or anyone else. I also have three trees which are guardians of my flat when I am away, which is often. When I first moved in, I saw rays of light coming from each tree, forming a triangle of light around the house in which my flat is situated. I acknowledged the spirit of each tree, and when I go away I ask them to hold the light around the house. When I come back I say thank you.

When the storms took place that destroyed much of Kew Gardens, where I live, I had just returned from overseas. It was two in the morning and only on my way back from the airport did I have any idea of how vicious the winds were. I thought 'my' trees would fall right into the house, so I spent hours talking to them. I asked them to lean sideways, to bend with the gale rather than fight against it. Even though trees on either side toppled, tearing out chunks of pavement, leaving a trail of destruction as though bombs had gone off, my guardian trees survived intact.

A French friend, Henri, who has a forest around his house in Provence, goes every day to talk to a particular tree that tells him what to do when things go wrong. Trees, like everything else in nature, will talk to all of us if we listen. An illustration of this is provided by the sacred forest at St Beaume in Provence, leading up to the deep cave in the cliff face where Mary Magdalene is supposed to have spent the last thirty years of her life.

This sacred forest of tall trees of great presence, where hunting has always been forbidden, has been revered throughout the mists of time back to the pre-Christian eras of Druids, pagans and animists. Kings, queens and popes have climbed up through this cathedral of trees, especially around Christmas-time, to pay homage to Mary Magdalene. There are many such natural temples through the world, of configurations of boulders, rivers, forests and rocky bays which we can reconsecrate by our reverence and love. I have never liked to enter the forest of St Beaume without asking permission first, and saying thank you afterwards.

Honouring the Earth

One of the best ways we can all help to re-establish ecological balance is by honouring these natural landscape temples in this way. To take time to be still and listen in such places, as Henri does, will often give us the guidance we need. This guidance may well require us to change things, not just to accept them. In the past many spiritual prophecies concerning the future of a religious group were considered by the prophets who delivered their message to have failed if they came true. A prophecy or prediction was a warning, giving an opportunity for change.

*   *   *

The following speech by Chief Seattle was delivered to Isaac I. Stevens, the new Governor and Commissioner of Indian Affairs for the Washington Territories in December 1854.

The President in Washington sends words that he wishes to buy our land. But how can you buy or sell the sky? The land? The idea is strange to us. If we do not own the freshness of the air and the sparkle of the water, how can you buy them? Every part of the Earth is sacred to my people. Every shining pine needle, every sandy shore, every mist in the dark woods, every meadow, every humming insect. All holy in the memory and experience of my people.

We know the sap which courses through the trees as we know the blood that courses through our veins. We are part of the Earth and it is part of us. The perfumed flowers are our sisters.

The bear, the deer, the great eagle, these are our brothers.

The rocky crests, the juices in the meadow, the body heat of the pony, and man, all belong to the same family.

The shining water that moves in the streams and rivers is not just water, but the blood of our ancestors. If we sell you our land, you must remember that it is sacred.

Each ghostly reflection in the clear waters of the lakes tells of events and memories in the life of my people. The water's murmur is the voice of my father's father.

The rivers are our brothers. They quench our thirst. They carry our canoes and feed our children. So you must give to the rivers the kindness you would give to any brother.

If we sell you our land, remember that the air is precious to us, that the air shares its spirit with all the life it supports. The wind that gave our grandfather his first breath also received his last sigh. The wind also gives our children the spirit of life. So if we sell you our land, you must keep it apart and sacred, as a place where man can go to taste the wind that is sweetened by the meadow flowers.

Will you teach your children what we have taught our children? That the Earth is our mother? What befalls the Earth befalls all the sons of the Earth.

This we know: the Earth does not belong to man, man belongs to the Earth. All things are connected like the blood that unites us all. Man did not weave the web of life, he is merely a strand in it. Whatever he does he does to himself.

One thing we know: our God is also your God. The Earth is precious to him and to harm the Earth is to heap scorn on its creator. Your destiny is a mystery to us. What will happen when the buffalo are slaughtered? The wild horses tamed? What will happen when the secret corners of the forest are heavy with the scent of many men and the view of the ripe hills is blotted by talking wires? Where will the thicket be? Gone. Where will the eagle be? Gone. And what is it to say goodbye to the swift pony and the hunt? The end of living and the beginning of survival.

When the last Red man has vanished with his wilderness and his memory is only the shadow of a cloud moving across the prairie, will these shores and forests still be here? Will there be any of the spirit of my people left?

We love this Earth as a newborn loves its mother's heartbeat.

So, if we sell you our land, love it as we have loved it. Care for it as we have cared for it. Hold in your mind the memory of the land as it is when you receive it. Preserve the land for all children, and love it, as God loves us all.

As we are part of the land you too are part of the land. This Earth is precious to us. It is also precious to you. One thing we know: there is only one God. No man be he Red man or white man can be apart. We are brothers after all.

*   *   *

The ecological warnings given us today by such people as Jonathan Porritt (ex-Director of Friends of the Earth), Jeremy Rifkin, Rupert Sheldrake, Helen Caldicott, David Bellamy and many others, including the indigenous peoples worldwide, appear to have a similar base. They urge us to wake up, to stop the exploitation and destruction of the Earth and its atmosphere, to recognise that short-term solutions, like sticking a Band-Aid on an amputated leg, simply do not work, and to accept responsibility and act.

Despite their seemingly pessimistic view of the world, most of these ecological prophets of doom also explain how we can repair the damage. We must stop burning fossil fuels, killing animals for food, stripping nature of its sacred value. We must drop our addiction to unnecessarily sophisticated luxury products, as well as drugs, alcohol and tobacco, and go back to the simple way of life. We must educate our children for the twenty-first century and not the 1800s.

Many of today's children are completely removed from nature. For example, hundreds of children in London had no idea that milk bought in cartons from a supermarket came originally from a cow. When introduced to the process of milking, many of them started to faint. We must dissolve such barriers of ignorance, just as we must wipe out those between races, nationalities, colours, classes and creeds. We should attempt to use our commonsense to avoid waste.

David Bellamy described how one of the biggest companies in Germany gives its workers free bus and train tickets as an incentive to leave their cars at home. As a result, the company not only helps to prevent environmental pollution, but also saves money by not having to build parking lots on site. His accountants, said Bellamy, discovered that, by setting light-reflectors on office lights, they save £485,000 in electricity bills every year. He explained that there was enormous investment potential in cleaning up the environment, and that maybe it was this realisation of, 'Oh my God, there's money in ecological awareness!' that would finally push big companies to act in environmentally sensitive ways.

Most environmentalists talk about returning to traditional methods of land care which, developed by indigenous peoples for thousands of years, are in complete harmony with the Earth. There is an immense wealth of wisdom in indigenous peoples, especially that which is being recognised in the American Indians and Australian Aboriginals, which we should tap into. David Bellamy did not advocate a return to the land as a retrograde step, but as a modern way to manage the world's natural resources. In discussing current problems he said that it was only through communities working, thinking and talking together, that these problems would be overcome. All we need is the will to act. Clearly, some of the possible solutions are going to force us to make choices about our current and future lifestyles.

For most of us, this means we must explore ways in which we can simplify our lives and become collectively more self-sufficient. We must ask ourselves: 'Do I have a God-given right to eat the flesh of animals bred on battery-farms who in most cases are killed with unbelievable cruelty?'

Releasing animals' spirits

In the 1970s I worked with a great teacher, Alan Chadwick. Alan had been a Shakespearean actor before he became a gardener and spiritual teacher. He created magnificent gardens all over the world, and taught his students the philosophy of life through nature and the garden. No student was allowed to eat meat unless he or she was prepared to kill the animal. Most of his students became vegetarians, but he showed those who chose not to how to kill a chicken or a sheep with consciousness, with love. This means we talk to the spirit of the animal first, tell it what we are about to do, and thank it. When this is done the spirit of the animal leaves its body before it is killed.

When one animal kills another, there are special devas – or angels – belonging to the animal kingdom who anaesthetise it. Our system of meat production and mass slaughterhouse murder interferes with this process and causes the animal's body to fill with fear, thus creating toxins which in turn affect our bodies when we eat unconsciously butchered meat. Muslims understand these truths. Their *halal* meat means that the animal has been killed in a specific and merciful way, to allow its spirit to escape.

We can alleviate some of this by blessing our food and offering our bodies as a means of transmutation to another level of every kind of food we eat, not just meat. Fifteen years ago I was involved with a group of doctors who decided to test the effects of various methods of cooking on foods. These experiments included frying, grilling, baking, use of microwave ovens, as well as the use of aluminium foil, and of blessing food once prepared. Microwave ovens tended to kill the life-force, aluminium foil markedly to diminish it, while blessing food restored much of its vitality. To pass a crystal over food either while cooking it or before eating it has the same effect. Similar benefits follow if we cook with care and love.

Making a start

We must also ask ourselves if we have the right to ski in the alps, if our presence there, and the building of elaborate hotels and ski-lifts, help to create erosion, which in turn causes avalanches that destroy even more trees, and subsequently the air we breathe. Do we have an automatic right to use cars so excessively, when we know that the resultant pollution adds to thermal heat expansion, one of the causes of our currently fluctuating weather patterns, and a possible cause of melting ice-caps, rising sea levels, and future tidal waves?

In other words, making choices about our current and future lifestyles means we must become totally aware of the laws of cause and effect. It also means our moving from individuality – I – (illness begins with i) to universality – we (wellness begins with we). It is not always possible to change everything at once, especially if we have forgotten that our limited human consciousness has powers once accorded to the gods. We can start by recognising that each one of us can make a difference and that the time is ripe for us to do so.

Aside from practical decisions, such as not to waste food, to pass on unused items of clothing, goods and utensils, and sometimes to walk instead of riding by car, we can all help to transform the environment by picking up litter where we find it in front of us – especially when it is a Coca-Cola can or discarded sweet wrapper half way up a mountain, or in the grass when we walk the dog. We can decide to admire wild flowers and leave them there for the next person to admire too, instead of picking them.

Water: the blood of Gaia

In Bulgaria, the students of Beinsa Douna were taught never to pass a mountain stream or spring without making sure that the water ran freely. They learned that water was sacred, the blood of Gaia or Mother Earth, and that it contained within it elements to heal mind, body and spirit. During one of my own visits to Bulgaria I developed altitude sickness in the mountains. Two of Beinsa Douna's women disciples, now eight-five years old, came to my tent and, through gestures, because we did not understand one another's languages, urged me to take off my clothes and to drink pints of hot water while they massaged me from head to foot with more hot water.

I began to feel even worse, but the two women insisted on pouring more water down my throat while they frenziedly rubbed my body. Eventually they wrapped me in blankets and told me to relax and try to sleep. I sweated and dozed, dozed and sweated. The women returned and administered more of their hot water treatment. They did this three times, after which I recovered completely.

I have seen and experienced water used as a healing treatment hundreds of times. For colds, 'flu, and even emotional depression, the same treatment was applied. Cold water compresses, such as ice wrapped in a face cloth, were applied to the wound or broken bone, followed immediately by hot water. This alternating therapy will release the muscle spasm often caused by pain.

Drinking warm water first thing in the morning and last at night not only clears the blood and organs of the body, but also clears away any blockage between our physical and etheric bodies. I used to suffer from migraine headaches and, apart from dealing with the cause (conflict with authority, my own as well as others') I found that to apply a wet pad, as hot as I could bear it, over my eyes and forehead, released the tension by relaxing the constriction of the blood vessels in the area that caused pain.

To drink lots of water is a simple way of clearing our bodies of toxicity and will, I believe, be acknowledged as the major medicine of the future. To revere water means not only to be aware of how we use it, and what it can be used for, but also to be willing to clear streams, ponds, fountains and rivers when they become blocked. As when releasing a constriction in the physical body, or the circulation, by doing this we help the Earth's energy to circulate more freely. We are also then more attuned to the present Age of Aquarius, whose sign is the waterbearer.

Healing the inner and outer worlds

Jonathan Porritt says: 'Ecology is a process of healing, a way of providing meaning to an otherwise sterile and empty world . . .'. No matter how simple the first ecological steps we take are (and of course there are hundreds more than the ideas I have mentioned) they will help us to move beyond our material confines, and recognise that we are strands in a miraculous web of creation connected to the source of life itself.

When we live this awareness, we jump into the magical world of quantum living, thinking and being. This quantum leap into another reality is not only an expansion of consciousness that recognises oneness in all of creation, but also dissolves the barriers between the visible and invisible, time and space, spirit and matter. Similar to the awakening of Kundalini consciousness, through its leap of energy from the base to the crown chakras, quantum thinking steps up life on to its next evolutionary level, gives birth to what Jean Houston called 'the Possible Human' and Paul Solomon described as 'the Meta-Human'. Both are descriptions of men and women who have thrown off the shackles of past conditioning, the brainwashing that said that there was only one way to think, which did not include imagination, intuition and inspiration.

Great scientists and inventors, such as Edison, Einstein and Tesla, many musicians, writers and artists have all demonstrated the qualities of the Possible and Meta human being, who easily moves far beyond what was previously considered normal. The Tibetan lamas, who can sit naked in the snow and melt it by using the power of their minds and imagination, bilocate – appear in many different places at once – and cover huge distances by leaping through the air, also demonstrate these qualities.

St Teresa, among many other saints, was an exceptional human being. She could levitate, and had visions which inspired her to live in a certain way. One day one of her nuns, while scrubbing the chapel floor, floated up to the ceiling. St Teresa sharply called her back, saying: 'This is not an excuse to get out of scrubbing the floor!' All these people were quantum thinkers who, in mastering the laws of time and space, recognised that there were no limitations to what a human being could do or be, provided his belief was strong enough.

Edison used to fast and go without sleep for days in order to reach a point of light-headedness in which the answers he needed would come. Einstein lulled himself into a similar state by gazing at clouds, while Tesla not only saw ideas in the air but wrote them there himself when he needed to remember them. Today we do not even need to make special efforts to attain this new level of creativity. The current epoch is already pushing us into it.

Nuclear evolution

In the 1960s Christopher Hills, PhD, author of *Nuclear Evolution* and many other books, used this title to describe the evolution of consciousness, the development of the human mind to its fullest potential, and the recognition that human consciousness affects the atomic, molecular structure of the universe.

Nuclear evolution is another way to describe quantum thinking, or the way that energy follows thought, and shows us that we not only create our own reality, but that with a snap of the imagination, can change it. To live in this way is similar to living inside a hologram. We see the whole picture instead of part of it. It is like being the writer, producer and director of a movie with an overview of the plot, instead of being stuck in the role of an actor in it. If we decide it is not going to be a box-office success, we can re-write the script.

To understand that we have the power to change whatever we do not like about our present circumstances is tremendously exciting. It is also frightening, because of the responsibility it brings. In the brilliant Dave Clark musical *Time*, Akash, played by Laurence Olivier, says: 'Look at what you are thinking. See the pettiness and the envy and the greed and fear, and all the other attitudes that cause you pain and discomfort ... If you truly want to change your world, my friends, you must change your thinking.'

Visualising the new world into being

Outside world events are simply a reflection of our internal states of mind. Our thoughts have creative power, which in the past we have used or directed unconsciously. The new world we are stepping into is one in which the power of thought and imagination, the inter-relatedness between consciousness and matter, will be demonstrated and worked with.

This means that no matter how dismal the current state of the world is, we have the power to change it without even getting out of bed. To know this is more important than any other discovery we have made. In other words, if we give some time and energy to managing and directing our consciousness towards the positive instead of the negative, we can turn the world around. To do this, we should focus on whatever may concern us, and visualise or imagine it in a different light.

For example, if we are worried about certain animals becoming extinct, we should see them as healthy and happy, adapting to a changing world instead of being annihilated by it. We ought, however, to remember that every few thousand years it may be that some species have completed their cycle of evolution on this planet, like the dinosaur. We should bless them, love them, and release them, in the same way as we might do when someone close dies.

Instead of feeling horror at what the Israelis and Arabs, or Serbs and Muslims are doing to one another, we should visualise them making friends, and send thoughts of peace, forgiveness and compassion towards anyone who fights a war, visualising them becoming tired of hurting one another, and moving forward into a new era of understanding and co-operation.

Instead of worrying about holes in the ozone layer, it is better to imagine them knitting together, after we have taken all possible practical steps to aid this. Maybe we should look at the possibility that these holes symbolise a need for us to open windows in our mind to an awareness of other planets and galaxies, thus moving towards a cosmic, instead of our merely individualistic, consciousness. Think of government and other leaders making decisions that benefit the whole of mankind instead of small nationalistic parts of it. Whether it is a dying species, a starving population, warring factions, disaster victims, governments or Earth changes that affect us, we can still do something about it, even from a distance.

O Great Spirit whose voice I hear in the winds
whose breath gives life to the world – hear me.
I am small and weak
I need your strength and your wisdom.

May I walk in beauty.
May my eyes ever behold the red and purple sunset.

Make my hands respect the things you have made
and my ears sharp to hear your voice.
Make me wise so that I may know
the things you have taught your children
the lessons you have hidden in every leaf and rock.

Make me strong, not to be superior to my brothers,
but to be able to fight my greatest enemy . . . myself.
Make me ever ready to come to you with straight eyes
so that when life fades as the fading sunset
my spirit will come to you without shame.

PRAYER OF THE SIOUX PEOPLE

Another potent exercise is to visualise the planet encircled with light, or to offer it, and everything and everyone on it, into the hands of God, with the thought that all is unfolding exactly as it should, whether we, from our relatively limited human perspective, can understand it or not. The Earth is the greatest school of all time, providing billions of different lessons and opportunities. It is a planet of duality, which teaches us the positive through the negative; if I need to learn to value my health, I may choose to occupy a body that is sick. If I need to appreciate peace, I may do so through war; freedom through years of imprisonment.

We can also do a tremendous amount, both individually and collectively, through prayer; simply say: 'Thy will be done!' A beautiful prayer for these times is the well-known Great Invocation:

> *From the point of Light within the mind of God*
> *Let light stream forth into the minds of men.*
> *Let Light descend on Earth.*
>
> *From the point of Love within the Heart of God*
> *Let love stream forth into the hearts of men.*
> *Let Christ return to Earth.*
>
> *From the centre where the Will of God is known*
> *Let purpose guide the little wills of men –*
> *The purpose which the Masters know and serve.*
>
> *From the centre which we call the race of men*
> *Let the Plan of Love and Light work out.*
> *And may it seal the door where evil dwells.*

Let Light and Love and Power restore the Plan on Earth.

Instead of watching TV in an empty-minded way, we could practise doing so consciously. In other words, project loving thoughts towards the actors, announcers and newscasters;

imagine that all the people who watch and listen benefit in some way.

The power of thought is limitless. I once worked in America with Olga Worrell, a well-known healer, in experiments to test her mental force. In front of my and others' eyes, she changed and dissolved cloud formations, appreciably improved the quality of food, water and wine, and made plants grow faster and bigger. Every one of us has something of this power. If we used it together, we could achieve miracles.

Even individually, right on our own, we can do wonders with the power of our thought. Anne, the eighteen-year-old daughter of a friend of mine who lived in Africa, was alone in the house one night when she was awakened by the noise of people breaking in. Too afraid to go downstairs to telephone for help, she crawled under her bed and prayed. She also strongly visualised white light surrounding both herself and the house. Hours later, when her parents returned, they found the door and windows of the house shattered. Anne was safe, and nothing in the house had been stolen.

The police eventually arrived, following reports from other houses in the area that a local gang was on the rampage. The police contingent very quickly traced and arrested the gang. When asked why they had robbed all the houses in the neighbourhood except this one, they replied that, as they started to break in, a huge shining wall rose up in front of them. It was so formidable that, frightened out of their wits, they ran away.

This is a true story, which clearly illustrates the great power of directed consciousness.

The invocations of the Essenes

Many spiritual groups before us have had this mastery. Edmond Bordeaux Szekely's book *The Gospel of the Essenes*, which he translated from the original Hebrew and Aramaic of the Dead Sea Scrolls, says that there are three paths leading to truth. The first is the path of consciousness, the second that of nature, and the third the path of accumulated experience of earlier generations, passed down through literature, art and music. He says, like many scientists and biologists today, that consciousness is the most immediate reality for us which contains the keys to the universe.

The Essenes were a brotherhood particularly strong in the last centuries before Christ and the first century AD. They lived simple lives on the shores of lakes and rivers, grew their own food, studied the laws of healing, astrology and prophecy. They were physically strong and psychologically healthy. Basic to the Essene way of life was their daily communion with the heavenly Father and earthly Mother, which they did by attunement through a special angel dawn and dusk. The evening angel was connected to the heavenly Father and the morning one to the earthly Mother.

I have practised and shared these daily invocations for at least thirty years, and found them to be a beautiful, simple and powerful way of moving through the week. The Essene tree of life sets out these angelic forces, beginning with Friday night, as follows:

Friday night		The Father and I are one
Saturday	a.m.	Greetings to the earthly Mother
	p.m.	Angel of Eternal Life
Sunday	a.m.	Angel of Earth (Regeneration)
	p.m.	Angel of Work and Creativity
Monday	a.m.	Angel of Life
	p.m.	Angel of Peace
Tuesday	a.m.	Angel of Joy
	p.m.	Angel of Power
Wednesday	a.m.	Angel of Sun
	p.m.	Angel of Love
Thursday	a.m.	Angel of Water
	p.m.	Angel of Wisdom
Friday	a.m.	Angel of Air

The Essenes also communed with the stars, trees, nature,

the different phases of the moon, and the spiritual brother-hood of the Children of Light. To invoke these angelic forces as they did is another way of helping to restore the relation-ship between Heaven and Earth, and will strengthen, guide and spiritually sustain us, so that instead of feeling like strangers in a foreign land we can enjoy the wonders of creation.

Part Three

THE MAGIC OF CREATIVE LIVING

10

OUT OF
THE SHADOWS

To move fully into the magical world of creative living, and to enjoy its wonders, we must drastically alter our perceptions of reality, and drop the crippling thought-patterns of the past, which have caused us to feel separate, isolated and helpless.

We have to stop looking at everyday life as if it were the only reality. The pictures flickering on the screens of our mind are no longer the only truth. Our situation is like that of a child who watches a movie and sees it as absolutely real, instead of a projection of celluloid images on a screen. As an adult he recognises the source of the scene, the rehearsals and dress-rehearsals of words and actions, that are finally reflected before him like a mirror-image of what was originally set in motion.

In his *Republic* Plato describes people who, living inside a cave, could only see shadows reflected on a wall by the flickering flames of a fire, which they assumed to be real. Eventually some of them leave the cave and go outside, where they see a different world, which includes shadows on the ground from the sun, and ultimately the sun itself. Full of excitement, they rush back to tell the others all about what they have discovered, only to be laughed at and told they are crazy. Those within the cave prefer to be imprisoned or chained by their illusions of what is real. It is safe, comfortable, and familiar.

Awakening to change in the 1990s means that we must break the chains that bind us to the conviction that we are born miserable sinners full of guilt, fear and self-contempt. Like the people imprisoned in Plato's cave, most of us are so afraid of life itself that we only just exist, trapped in a shadow-land that is so stifling that we never claim our right to live fully and joyously. The new epoch drags us by the scruff of our necks out of this shadow-land and into one of play, excitement and adventure.

Lack of self-love

During my counselling sessions I have found that the basic common denominator to the problems that beset humanity is lack of self-love. It is the prime saboteur of human happiness – the wound that can create dysfunctional people who reach for drugs and alcohol to numb the pain. If we do not love and accept ourselves, nothing works. We blame others for what goes wrong in our lives, put the responsibility for our happiness and unhappiness on other people, try to be what we imagine they want us to be, instead of accepting ourselves exactly the way we are.

When we live like this it is not only sad, but exhausting, as if we were blowing up a life-size balloon, and had to keep it full of air. Every now and then we get distracted, and look away, which causes the balloon to deflate, so we frantically puff more air into it. This balloon of 'false image' comes from the fear that who I really am *is* who I fear I really am. In other words, I am not so crash-hot as a personality, so I had better create a nicer me. This separates us from our real selves, from life, from people and happiness. It is time to let the balloon deflate itself and fly away.

Much of our lack of self-worth stems from the fact that

parents tend to give love to their children when their behaviour and performance fits the parents' demands, and withdraw that love when they do not. This teaches us that love, acceptance or approval are conditional on how we behave or perform, instead of being unconditional for who we are.

Whether parents or not, how many of us freely let the people in our lives be who they are, and not what we want them to be? How many of us say, 'I'll love you, provided you love me'? Or 'I'll love you provided you conform to what I demand that you do' – such as come home on time for the delicious meals I prepare, weed the garden, empty the rubbish, and pay all the bills' – or, from the husband's viewpoint, to have prepared delicious meals on time, to take care of the children, to dress seductively at all times, and to be an unfailing source of support.

Unconditional love is the recognition in the other of the divine. It does not mean acceptance of conscious and consistent cruelty by others, but rather to separate a person from what he or she does. In other words, the divine in me acknowledges the divine in you, even if I do not always like or approve of what you do.

Most religions teach us that self-love leads to egotism, yet without self-love we do not have the confidence to enjoy life, make mistakes and correct them without punishing ourselves, or love others easily, without fearing that our love will not be returned. Religion also teaches us that we are all sparks of God and therefore perfect, while at the same time filling us with fear and guilt for being miserable sinners. To love and accept ourselves totally as we are now does not mean that there is no room for future improvement. However, we have no need to seek excessive perfection, any more than we should condemn ourselves too ruthlessly. We should live comfortably in the middle, perfectly whole, not wholly perfect.

Orthodox religion often injects guilt in children. For example, my convent school education taught me that I was the worst child ever born and that God was a bad-tempered, judgemental, and terrifying old man with a beard, who had nothing better to do day and night but to peer accusingly at me from the clouds, where he chalked up all my transgressions. I was told that the good died young, because God loved them and wanted to live with them. I would therefore live to a ripe old age. I learnt that I was the rotten apple who would contaminate all the other apples, and would inexorably end up living at the devil's right hand.

During one particularly difficult term I was discovered with a book entitled *Beauty Hints from the Stars* which I had secreted between the covers of my mathematics exercise book. I was locked up in the Mother Superior's study for three days while every nun who taught in the school, as well as the two hundred from the convent, came one by one to tell me what an evil and unforgivable sinner I was.

In fact, the book had a picture of Marilyn Monroe on the cover, and the beauty tips inside were of a fairly innocuous nature. They revealed that Lana Turner rubbed her elbows with lemon rinds, Doris Day washed her hair with camomile tea, while Marilyn Monroe herself used cucumber face masks to keep her skin looking good. It was only years later that I discovered that Marilyn Monroe was thought to be wicked because she had dared to pose naked for a photo – although she certainly was not naked in this book.

This convent school indoctrinated me with the belief that no matter what I did I was an instrument of the devil and would 'come to no good'. The nuns instilled in me a paralysing fear of authority and of making mistakes, as well as such a deep sense of guilt, that even today I am often the one who apologises when someone else pushes a supermarket trolley over my feet, or drops tea over my skirt. In the past I used to be the sort of person who would come home from a hard day's work, sit down to catch my breath, and if my son or husband came into the room, leap to my feet, apologise for just sitting, and explain that I was just about to prepare dinner, water the garden, or walk the dog.

If someone said: 'You look wonderful, what a pretty dress!'

instead of saying 'Thank you' I would apologise, describe the bags under my eyes, and add that I had bought the dress ten years ago secondhand. I had so little self-worth that I virtually apologised for the air I breathed. Guilty people become perfectionists. They explain, justify and apologise for every action they take. Unable to give love and approval to themselves, they seek it from others, and often end up in the 'poor little me' martyr syndrome, while life passes them by.

I am sure that the nuns at my convent genuinely believed that by making me feel guilty they improved my character. In fact, as Paul Solomon says, if guilt is made obsessional, by far its most likely effect is to make the sufferer commit exactly the same supposed crime again. If guilt has any virtue at all, it is simply to give us a little nudge, a tap on the shoulder, to point out that we have made a mistake. There is no sense in using guilt for self-destruction. Yet many of us, myself included, have without reason been immobilised by guilt for most of our lives.

Fear, like guilt, can paralyse. Children need to learn to respect the fact that some things may harm them, such as fast traffic on highways, swimming-pools and high seas (especially if they cannot swim), fierce dogs or other hostile animals. Respect is very different from fear. Children who are taught to fear, in the belief that it protects them from what they fear, often lose their sense of adventure, their motivation to touch, taste and try. Parents can, by their own example rather than words, show their children that life does not have to be a series of worries about finance, health, safety and the future, but should be a miraculous and wonderful opportunity to grow and evolve. The following words from a poster entitled 'Children Learn What They Live' perfectly sums this up:

If a child lives with criticism, he learns to condemn.
If a child lives with hostility, he learns to fight.
If a child lives with ridicule, he learns to be shy.
If a child lives with shame, he learns to feel guilty.

If a child lives with tolerance, he learns to be patient.
If a child lives with encouragement, he learns confidence.
If a child lives with praise, he learns to appreciate.
If a child lives with fairness, he learns justice.
If a child lives with security, he learns to have faith.
If a child lives with approval, he learns to like himself.
If a child lives with acceptance and friendship, he learns to
find love in the world

In Khalil Gibran's book *The Prophet* he says in response to a woman's question about children:

Your children are not your children.
They are the sons and daughters of Life's longing for itself.
They come through you but not from you,
And though they are with you yet they belong not to you.

You may give them your love but not your thoughts,
For they have their own thoughts.
You may house their bodies but not their souls,
For their souls dwell in the house of tomorrow, which you
cannot visit, not even in your dreams.
You may strive to be like them, but seek not to make them
like you . . .

The lost inner child

No matter how far removed our childhood was from these ideals, most of us had parents who did the best they could for us at the time. Most of us who have children do likewise. We fall into parenting without training or qualification, so despite how perfect we may try to be, or how happy our family life is or was, there will usually be something missing. We tend to identify more with the something missing, or what was not there in the form of love, care and support, than with what *was* there. The result is that many of us have an inner 'lost child' who, angry, afraid, unhappy or forgotten, clamours for attention, and demands that all its unfulfilled needs from the past are taken care of. This inner child's hunger for love can affect, and even destroy – if ignored – the balance of our lives today.

My own lost inner child, believing it could never win, stimulated the desire in me to prove I could. Consequently I worked almost 20 hours a day for months at a time, until this neglected child, who needed some play and fun, rebelled. I would then collapse in a heap, throw up my 'responsible' job – which was usually creative and enjoyable, as well as highly competitive – and loll about on the beach until lack of money pushed me back on to the same treadmill. I was never able to balance work and play – it was either all one or all the other.

In addition to the nagging inner-child syndrome, this pattern is also a part of not trusting one's animus or male energy, which we use to accomplish everything in life. It is active, assertive, outgoing, whereas the anima or feminine energy is receptive and in-going. If we do not trust the inner male, we can become hardworking perfectionists, trying to compensate for our inadequacy, or start-stopping people who never complete what they begin. Mistrust of the inner woman usually results in people cut off from, or denying the value of, feelings, imagination and intuition.

In my case I then did something that shocked me out of this pattern. I was writing a three-days-a-week page for a newspaper. I had carte blanche to write on any subject that came into my head. This was tremendously exciting and terrifying. I had two secretaries to whom I was meant to dictate my copy. I found I could not dictate without writing my ideas down first, so I stayed up most of the night working out what to dictate the following day. I worked seven days a week all day and half the night, in terror of failure.

Six months later my totally unrecognised inner child said: 'I've had enough of this!' and threw a tantrum. I found myself in the editor's office handing in my resignation. At home, I went into complete shock at what I had done. I felt as if I'd almost been possessed by another personality. For days, I sat and thought about my life, and suddenly a little voice in my head said: 'How old is the child in you now?' The number 6 popped up, and, closing my eyes, I saw in my imagination myself at six, curled up in a heap on a lawn, quivering with fear and apprehension, having been deposited in a boarding school with no explanation.

I felt the person I was at that moment merge with this little girl from the past, and I cried all the tears I was too afraid to cry on the lawn. I then imagined taking this child in my arms and talking to her. I told her I was very sorry that I had never before explained how much I loved her, that she was part of me and my life, and that we would spent lots of time together. We would play and have fun, meet people, travel, explore, learn, grow, and share things with each other.

Visualisations for the inner child

I stressed that I was *always* available to her, and that she could say anything to me, whether she was happy or sad, what she liked or disliked, and I would do the same with her. I imagined running outside with her on to a beautiful sunny beach. We splashed in the sea, collected shells, drew pictures in the sand, hurled sticks in the air for passing dogs to catch. I visualised our wandering through overgrown gardens, smelling the flowers, rolling in the grass, climbing trees, paddling in pools and streams, playing with kittens, ducks, ponies and puppies. I left her sitting on a swing with a kitten in one hand and a puppy in the other, and opened my eyes to find myself back in the present.

During the following days I did this visualisation exercise many times. I often began by asking myself 'How old is the child in me today?' As the six-year-old healed the numbers changed, to 8 or 3 or 14. Often a forgotten memory of something that had happened during one of these years would also pop up. As I dealt with each incident and fed this child in her inner reality, she stopped demanding attention from me in mine. I suddenly realised that I could not only heal the child, by giving her the love and assurance she felt she had missed out on, but I could also heal the past, by using my imagination to re-create what had really happened. I saw that my past influenced me but should not control me. And so it is for all of us.

Using the power of imagination and fantasy – the Greek word *phantasia* means to make visible the invisible – we can explore every facet of ourselves, delve into our pain, our fears, phobias and traumas, and re-create our past, just as the editor of a book, film or play cuts out what does not work. The old age said that emotional healing was a life-long process which required a well-trained counsellor. The Quantum age, while not dismissing the well-trained counsellor, says that instant change, in all areas of our lives, from health to relationships to self-image, is possible, the magic wand being the power of the mind and imagination, through which we can work miracles.

There are dozens of different ways of getting in touch with and healing the inner child. Among those I have found the most successful are the following.

Visualisation I: Meeting your inner child

Close your eyes and imagine yourself walking through trees into a glade, where you will find your inner child. This child may appear as male or female, baby or adolescent, obedient or rebellious, sad or happy. Before speaking, take a moment to assess what you see, how you feel, what the child thinks and feels about him or herself, life, and you. Decide what this child most needs from you to be healthy and happy, and give it in abundance. Do not forget to give love, approval, support and reassurance, as well as asking forgiveness for not having done so before.

This type of exercise can free us from much of what is unconscious imprisonment to the past. You may want to substitute a room in a house for that glade, or imagine removing from the child's shoulders bricks that symbolise the weights of suffering unwillingly borne. The key to success in inner work, whether it be to heal the child, find the shadow or communicate with angels and guides, is to let the imagination play, and see what happens. Whether through visions, symbols, words or colours we are always shown exactly what we need to see.

Visualisation II: Your outer and inner self

Another simple but effective exercise is to imagine walking into a room where you also find a child. You notice it, but walk past it, through a door into another room, where you find a second child. Take time to compare the second child with the first. Is it older or younger, male or female, shy and withdrawn or smiling and happy? Most important of all, how does this second child respond to your presence? If you smile and hold out your hand, does it smile too, or shrink back in fear? The first child symbolises our outer self, the second the inner or hidden personality. At different times in our lives one or the other will appear dominant.

There is no right or wrong, better or worse in this exercise. It is simply a way of discovering whether your inner or outer self in the moment is the most happy and free. Having seen and compared the two, which often releases a great deal of repressed emotion, we must sense their reaction to each other, reassure and love them before taking them out of the house and releasing them to play together in the sun. When you do this you strengthen both inner and outer aspects of personality.

Extending visualisation

Visualisation exercises such as these can be used to change and heal almost any aspect of our lives, especially things we may dislike or fear to do. By involving our inner senses we radically sharpen our perceptions and powers in the outer world. To lose weight, win a race, climb a mountain or pass a test, see yourself doing it first in your mind's eye. The more you practise, the easier you will find it is to do whatever it is that you want to do.

A friend of mine who was a ballet-dancer fell in love with, and subsequently married, a circus trapeze artist. Not wanting to live the kind of life where their work kept them apart, she decided to partner him on the trapeze. Very frightened of heights, she found the initial training almost impossible, until she began to use visualisation as part of the training. Three times a day she closed her eyes and imagined herself balanced on the high wire, performing incredible acrobatics with ease. She flew through the air from wire to wire, hung by her teeth and juggled balls as she pirouetted on the wire. To her amazement, this inner practice motivated her finally to climb the ladder up to the real wires in the circus tent, and begin her training in earnest. She said: 'I was still afraid, but something inside impelled me to feel the fear and do it anyway.'

No actor would dream of performing on stage without having rehearsed his part many times. Dreams, guided fantasies and reveries, in which we actively use our imagination, enable us all to rehearse as often as we like whatever parts we want to play next. We should remember that all such exercises work better if we relax the body first, by methods such as breath control or by tensing each muscle one by one from top to toe. A third way is to visualise light or colour washing through every part of our body.

In workshops in which I use guided imagery to help people face and explore many aspects of themselves (both from this and other lives) I use all three methods as part of an overall preparation which deepens the experience.

Visualisation downwards and upwards

I have also found it helps, when exploring the unconscious and subconscious, to imagine going down rather than up. This can be done in various ways too. We can count backwards from 21 to zero, descend a flight of stairs or steps, float down a hill, a slope, a rainbow, or even imagine stepping on an escalator or taking a lift. The downward descent may lead into a cave, dungeon or cellar, but is useful imagery if we want to find and heal our unconscious blocks, our shadow or sub-personality selves. We may not know what lies buried or hidden, but the willingness to go down into the depths can put us in touch with, and release, an energy that may present a hiccup in our lives today.

To explore higher levels of consciousness, to communicate with angels, teachers and guides, to align ourselves with our higher or overviewing soul selves, read our own Akashic records, or find our Book of Life, we should go up rather than down. To do this, we should imagine lifting the life force out of our bodies from toe to top, concentrating on each part from feet through ankles, calves, shins, knees, pelvis, chest, shoulders, neck, to the head and everything in between, as if there were a magnet at the top of our skull that drew our energy up. We can imagine this energy or force like a balloon no longer tied to our physical body, but free to drift and float. We can see it lifting higher and higher, up and up into other realms of consciousness where we may find and speak with healers, teachers and guides who can give us insight into ourselves.

Moving into and out of a visualisation

Because some of us find visualisation difficult, especially when we begin, it is better if we create a backdrop for these meetings, by imagining an ancient temple or library, a special room or even a cave, where we can picture ourselves taking the hand of our mentor or guide, rather than try to force a clear picture. We must not be afraid to ask questions, even if the only image we have is of yellow or brown or green spots before our eyes, instead of a sense of someone being there. Our intent to communicate with what is really our own inner wisdom always brings results.

However, instead of 'flashing lights in the sky' as answers to what we are desperate to know, the replies may pop up through the books we read, the radios we switch on, or the conversations we overhear while travelling to work. Some of us intuitively sense things rather than clairvoyantly see them. These can include words, symbols, shapes, colours and numbers, as well as people we have known or never seen before. To learn the language of both the inner and the higher self is similar to learning the language of dreams. It requires, like learning any other language, practice, humour and perseverance.

We should also remember that, however enjoyable it may be to float off into a different reality, and even if we want to stay there, we must bring ourselves back to the physical body before opening our eyes.

To do this, all we need is to reverse the imagery, float down rather than up. We can simply imagine the same bubble or balloon of consciousness or life-force drifting slowly and easily down until it rests on the top of our heads, when we can absorb it back into our bodies. We can then breathe it into the face, head and shoulders, into and through every cell, muscle, tissue, and organ until we feel it anchored in our feet, and follow this by sighing, stretching, and pressing our feet to the floor until we feel ready to open our eyes. If we do not take the time and trouble to do this, we can feel disorientated and light-headed.

11

FREEDOM FROM
PAIN AND FEAR

Journal writing

Another more external way of delving into our past in order
to face our future is through journal writing. Initiates in the
schools of Ancient Wisdom, the schools of esoteric learning,
sometimes known as Mystery Schools, learned how to move
freely between past, present and future, visible and invisible
realms, by using their imagination. Many of the visualisation
techniques we use today have come down to us from these
ancient schools. These are now available to all of us, instead
of just to the select few, and can help us to transform our lives.

The goal of the student in a mystery school was spiritual
growth, development of the personality, and perfection of the
character. Aside from inner work, each student was required
to keep a journal, recording the day's events, his reaction to
them, the effect of his prayers and the quality of his
meditations. Journal writing was a form of spiritual book-
keeping, a means of self-discovery and understanding, a map
of the soul's journey through life.

We can echo these teachings ourselves. To keep a journal in
which we record our dreams, note the people and qualities

they represent, the key events or situations with the most impact, our emotional reactions to all this, combined with our daily thoughts and perceptions, will bring insight to the surface of our waking minds that we may not have recognised before. To do this, note: 'Where am I now?' as if writing the title of a chapter in a book. 'How long have I been in this phase? What happened to put me there?'

For example, my child died, my husband or wife left home, I read a book or lost my job. It may be very simple or very dramatic. We can use journal writing to go back through our lives from now to birth, the best and worst moments, what was working for and against us, the people, good or bad, and their effect on our lives, our ideals, hopes, fears, dreams and recollections which, as we look back, influenced us in some way.

I began recording my dreams and thoughts when I was six years old. I could pour words into my diary as if into the ears of an intimate friend who was totally receptive to anything I said or did. As an adult, I found that the combination of inner work with journal writing brought my inner and outer life together, so that the outer confirmed the inner and vice versa. This synthesis helped me to interpret, not just my past, but also the daily life events that unfolded around me.

The result was that every waking hour was filled with excitement and curiosity. Paul Solomon gave some of the best journal workshops I have ever attended. He suggested that we divided our journal into seven sections. The first dealt with the past. The second was like a daily log. The third noted the cast of characters that appeared in our day, what they did and how we reacted to them. The fourth was a letter to our higher self or inner teacher. The fifth was to record our dreams. The sixth was to describe the day's lessons or challenges and our attitude to them. The seventh section was to note any insights or inspirational thoughts that came up during our meditation.

These seven sections also relate to the seven chakras or energy points of the body. The key to success with Paul's formula was not to write too much. Some people find it easier to draw pictures and symbols in their journals instead of writing.

Mapping out your early childhood

In workshops, I sometimes use the following technique to show the participants how best to understand the influences of their early childhoods. I ask them to draw a circle and put their name in the middle, and to write the names around the edge of everyone who played a role in their first seven years. By this, I mean those who were physically present, not Uncle Charlie or a twice-removed cousin who lived in Timbuktoo, who were part of the family but never seen. I then get the seminar members to draw straight lines from their name to the name of everyone who nurtured them – in the sense of changing their nappies, feeding and burping them, and wiping their noses.

They then draw wavy lines to those they felt comfortable and happy with, and jagged lines to those with whom they felt ill at ease and wary. It is possible to have all three types of lines going to the same person. I then suggest that the participants close their eyes and ask themselves: 'Who really loved me, exactly as I was, not because I made my bed, did my homework, or cut the grass or did the washing-up.

The answers can shock. John, in a workshop, realised that an old man he used to visit every day on his way home from school was the only person in his childhood who gave him total and unconditional acceptance, love and approval. He used to sit on the old man's knee, while they read books, looked at birds' eggs, and pored through old stamp albums together. One day his parents came to collect him, and leapt to the conclusion that their son was being molested. They dragged John off the old man's knee and, shouting abuse, threatened to call the police. John, aged seven, did not understand what the fuss was about. His parents gave him no further explanation, and forbade John ever to visit his friend again.

During this exercise John suddenly realised that a part of

him had frozen inside from that moment, and he wept. He also recognised that, despite feeling unloved by his parents, they did in fact love him, but did not show it. John healed his frozen inner child over a period of time through writing letters to the child of his past. He subsequently became a counsellor, specialising in children's problems.

Writing and drawing are powerful therapeutic tools, and can provide immediate cathartic relief. By emptying our feelings on to paper, we free ourselves of our pain and fear. We literally write or draw them out of our system.

Forgiveness

When we reflect on the past, no matter how we go about it, we often remember people we need to forgive. In fact, unwillingness to forgive, or to let go of old memories, is, like lack of self-love, one of the major blocks to happiness and success. During my adolescence, it suddenly occurred to me that the divine in me was able to do a lot that the 'poor little me' could not. I made up a number of affirmations that I used to repeat in my head when I felt insecure or unhappy. One of them was: 'I can, and will, through God. God can and will through me.'

I had a lot of forgiving to do too, so when my rage or frustration made it virtually impossible for me to forgive, I would imagine facing my then tormentor or oppressor, and saying to them, my teeth often clenched, 'Through the divine in me, I forgive the human in you and in me, which has caused this problem. Usually I did not feel an immediate wave of forgiveness flowing from me to the other person, but, on some level, and within a few days, it always worked. The barriers between us melted and we became friends again.

When we invoke the divine, in both ourselves and others, we reach up to the highest levels in ourselves, which is way beyond the struggling personality that holds on so tightly and refuses to let go.

As well as invoking the divine to help me to forgive, I used to write letters to the angels of people I was having difficulties with – 'Dear angel, of Tom, Dick or Mary, please help me deal with this situation – ' which I then went on to describe. At the end I said 'Thank you' and signed off 'With love, from Soozi'. This too always worked, as if it bypassed the unconscious resistance of the outer personality and was heard instead by their true essence. I still use this method to solve communication problems today. However, now, before signing off, I add, 'Please give me the right word, the opportunity and the courage to say them.' I then burn the letter in a candle flame. This is a form of written prayer. I have found it always succeeds.

Because I did this for years, I believed and felt that I had forgiven everyone in my life, including those who I felt had harmed me most. As I see it, true forgiveness, both of ourselves and others, means that we erase the memory of what happened so completely that it is as if it happened to someone else. In other words, 'the person I was, or they were then (whether from this or other lives) is not who I am or they are today.' We both have a different understanding and perspective, rather like an adult looking back at the child he was.

I later discovered that I had *not* in fact forgiven one particular person who was part of my painful childhood, although I had even believed that the karma was completed between us. In fact, when I heard the karmic chord between us snap, I collapsed on the floor with laughter. Soon afterwards I flew to Australia. On the way I became so ill that the immigration authorities assumed I had contracted a major infectious disease. Reluctant to let me into the country, they put me into quarantine for several days.

During this time I had a crisis similar to an NDE, or Near Death Experience, in which I found myself out of my body in what seemed to be an astral level. It was very dark, noisy and uncomfortable. Shadowy shapes brushed past me like cobwebs. I was very aware of the separation between myself and my body. I thought that if anyone found me like this they would think I was in a catatonic trance or had gone crazy, and would lock me up in a padded cell. Shivering and shaking, I thought I had gone crazy myself. Suddenly a figure appeared in front of me and said: 'Are you going to forgive X?'

Amazed, I replied: 'I have!' Three times I was asked the same question. Three times I replied that I had forgiven X. Suddenly I felt as if I had been struck on the head by an axe. I was cleft in half to the groin, where I discovered a raw bleeding wound, which was the accumulated pain of no love or support, and of childhood abandonment. I realised that I had forgiven X as much as I humanly could, but there was a residue. I began to weep and wail, to the extent of wanting to bang my head against the wall. Finally, and in fact three days later, this figure reappeared, and asked: 'Well, *are* you going to forgive X?' To my surprise, I heard myself saying that I wanted to, had tried to, but simply could not. This figure recoiled and, pointing a finger at me, said very sternly: 'I see. And you would condemn this entity to walk an astral level for eternity, yes?'

I realised at once that what he meant was the astral level similar to what some call purgatory. I was stunned. I had never realised that lack of forgiveness could put people in this terrible place. I thought of Hitler, and decided that I could not even condemn him to this purgatory, especially for eternity. 'Who am I?' I asked myself, 'to judge what anyone else does? It's all I can do to keep one foot after the other in dealing with my own life.' As these thoughts flew through my mind, I heard great sighs and groans fill the space around me. The ghostlike figures surrounding me tried to grab me, begging for help and release. They were desperate to live a physical life again and put right what they and others had done wrong.

However compassionate I felt, I could do nothing for them. I had the sensation of falling into and merging with my wound, and coming through it back into my body. Only then was I able totally to forgive X, with whom my relationship instantly changed. My understanding of forgiveness also changed. I realised that our refusal or resistance, both conscious and unconscious, to forgive, condemned not only others but also ourselves to this waste land. Many of use lose years, even many lives, chained to people we fear, hate and despise, while others are desperate to have the opportunity we have to be here on Earth now.

Forgiveness has always been a major factor in spiritual growth. As the consciousness of the planet lifts to another level, it is even more important than ever before. Our refusal to let go of the past literally chains us to it. We may think it easier to forgive once we are out of the physical body through death, and into another dimension, but, from all the descriptions of Near Death Experiences, this does not appear to be true. We get stuck with the very person we wanted to escape from, until we finally work through the problem. Aside from invoking the divine in us to forgive when the personality seems unable to, I have found the following exercise helpful.

Visualisation for cutting the cords

I close my eyes, and imagine following a path to a door, on the other side of which I am going to find the person I need or want to forgive. This may include my asking them for forgiveness too. I take a moment or two to reflect on what happened and how I reacted to it. How did I change and grow as a result of this experience? I open the door, and imagine the person in front of me. I first say exactly what I felt at the time, or what maybe I still feel now. It may include words of hate or despair.

Having got that off my chest, I take a few deep breaths, and look at the positive side. For example, my husband runs off with another woman and, after the initial shock and pain, I begin a new life which forces me to stand on my own two feet. I develop a strength and independence, an inner security which maybe I never had before. I then thank the person who was the catalyst for this, and ask to be shown the karmic bonds between us. These may appear in my mind's eye as thick ropes, bands of colour, silvery ribbons, threads or simply a sense of 'Yes, there's something there.'

I repeat my affirmation,

'Through the divine in me, I forgive the human in you and in me, and acknowledge the part you played in my life.' Using a sword, a knife, scissors or a candle-flame, or whatever else seems appropriate at the time, I cut through the cords. I mentally affirm: 'I cut these cords with the power of God.' When I sense that they are cut, I imagine my right hand on the navel of, first, the other person, and then of myself. I now say: 'I heal and seal this cord in the love of God.' I then release them to be what they truly are, and not who I want them to be. I imagine this person and myself surrounded by light, and, like an actor finishing a part in a play, therefore free to move on to something new. This is a particularly powerful method for changing and healing relationships with parents.

This does not mean that we sever all connection to them, but rather that we lift the relationship from the level of solar plexus to the heart. We then stop unconsciously pulling on one another. If we cut the cords in this way when strong emotional or sexual relationships came to an end, we would literally make a clean break and recover more easily. Relationships like these also create powerful psychic links which can stay with us long afterwards, leaving each of us vulnerable to the other. The type of exercise I have just described can also help us cut the cords that bind us to bad habits, past events, old memories of this and other lives, fears and apprehensions that continue to cause a hiccup in our progress today.

Fear of dying

All fears inhibit, but the fear of death is the greatest obstacle to living and the enjoyment of life. Western society conditions us to deny death as something catastrophic and unnatural.

The process of dying is usually associated with fear, anxiety and confusion. We fear pain and disease, of being incapacitated in some way, and therefore a liability to our families and friends. Fear of death includes the terror of letting go, of change, of the unknown, of leaving and losing everything that is loved and familiar. Many of us fear that we do not exist unless we are in a physical body, while others fear facing the consequences of what they have or have not done in life.

Selfishly, we dread the loss and loneliness caused by the death of someone we love. We usually whisper about death behind closed doors, as if it will go away like a bad dream if we refuse to acknowledge it. Yet we only have to look at nature to see that everything is constantly changing. Nothing is fixed, everything is impermanent. Nothing is born that does not die. A physical death is a spiritual birth, and the pangs of death a spiritual labour. By the same token, a physical birth is in a sense a spiritual death, a restriction of the consciousness we had before. Death and birth are neither a beginning nor an end, but part of the continuing cycle of creation. Each complements the other, and perhaps it takes confrontation with death to find the meaning of life.

Because I grew up with an awareness of other realities, and saw souls both in and out of the body, I had no fear of being physically dead. I believed, and still believe, in the continuity of life. Despite this, I had a great fear of the act of dying itself. I imagined that, no matter how we died, whether by accident, illness, violence or suicide, there would always be an unpleasant choking, a gasping for breath. I then had an NDE, which completely released me from this terror.

There was no sense of struggle. I found myself drawn through the top of my head out of my body and into a circle of white light, which was filled with a deep delphinium blue colour. Initially I felt as if I had popped out of clothes that were too tight. I had a sense of incredible expansion, freedom and excitement. I seemed to be floating, filled with peace and tranquillity. I remember thinking: 'If only people knew what it was like to die, they would not be so afraid.'

During this experience, I was shown that the only thing that really mattered in life, aside from living it to the full, was love; that lack of love, tolerance and kindness to one another was far worse than any major mistakes that we might consider that we had made. I saw that there were no mistakes. There were choices which led to different experiences, which would ultimately become part of our soul's wisdom and understanding.

I suddenly realised that I had expected judgement and punishment, but there was none, apart from how I judged and punished myself. I saw that at death we gain a wider perspective, but we do not immediately change consciousness as a result of no longer being in a physical body. I understood too that it was easier to deal with any 'unfinished business' *before* we died, rather than afterwards, and that we create our future astral or emotional body by the way we live today.

I had no sense of threat or coercion, but rather one of freedom and choice to do or be whatever I wanted. Drawn back into my body, I felt exhilarated as never before. I was free to explore, touch and taste everything life had to offer. Since then I have met and talked to hundreds of people across the world who have had similar experiences. Not only had they lost their fear of death and dying, so that they were more fully alive than ever before, but they also agreed that, in the words of Albert Schweitzer: 'The real tragedy of life is what dies inside a man while he lives.'

Khalil Gibran wrote:

You would know the secret of death.
But how shall you find it unless you seek it in the heart
of life?
The owl whose night-bound eyes are blind unto the day
cannot unveil the mystery of light.
If you would indeed behold the spirit of death, open your
heart wide unto the body of life.
For life and death are one, even as the river and the sea
are one.

As this century comes to an end, and we move into the next millennium, it is more essential than ever before that we drop the old fears of death which limit, bind and blind us. Death is an initiation, a ritual or rite that allows us to expand beyond the limitation of the physical body.

In ancient esoteric schools, initiates were placed inside a sarcophagus for days at a time, during which they were expected to leave their bodies, explore astral and other realms, and then return and report to their teachers all that they saw and discovered. The current flood of Near Death Experiences seems to me to be a replacement of these initiations, and, though not total proof of life after death, does provide some evidence for it. I believe that these NDEs are partly preparing us for a future when we shall operate in a much lighter and more etheric body.

This new body will enable us to raise or lower our vibrations, rather as we might change gears in a car, in order to move between planes without suffering our present often traumatic physical birth and death. We shall learn what we need to learn, do what we need to do, then move on. We shall participate much more consciously in the transition we today call death. Many people are already doing this, that is, neatly packing up all their affairs when they feel their hour has come, then lying down to die quite unmelodramatically.

Dion Fortune was a psychiatrist who died in 1945. She was also a famous mystic and occultist. Her last book was *Through the Gates of Death*. When she reached her last chapter she told her secretary that to make it authentic she needed to experience death herself. She then went off to her study. When her secretary followed her a few hours later, she found her dead on the floor. Dion Fortune then dictated the end of the book to her.

Our attitude to death governs our attitude to life. The fear of death frequently results in our failure to live life to its full potential. The present century has, through war, famine, earthquake and disease, brought death home to us on a scale perhaps never seen before, but which we are likely to see grow even greater in the future. Already AIDS, suicide, drugs and accidents add to this toll like a plague. We have to accept this, but not as a defeat. Instead we must bid those who die goodbye, as though they were going home after a visit to a foreign land. We know we shall miss them, but we let them move on to a new and different life without allowing our grief, pain or selfish desire to have them near us mar their joy. In fact, we should celebrate their return home, rather than mourn their departure.

Our reluctance to face death is similar to that in John Brantner's description: 'Like children playing games at twilight, we don't want to go home when we're called.' However, at this present time all over the world hundreds of young people are choosing to 'go home' long before we, who are left behind, may think it time for them to do so. Many of them have work to do after death, to help the Earth and all of us on it move through these times. Their brief lives were just a reminder to them of what physical life was like, but in order to fulfil their task they had to move on. Although most of these deaths are the result of accidents, many are suicides, which are increasing like an epidemic. From NDE research into attempted suicides, it seems that instead of feeling themselves drawn into the light, they felt enveloped into a grey foggy atmosphere created by the pain and confusion of those they had left behind. Many of these attempted suicides were so shocked by what they had done that they renounced any thought of trying again.

Sending light and love to the dying

We can help suicide victims by holding, in our mind's eye, an image of them surrounded by and filled with light. Even if we do not understand why they killed themselves, we can help to release them from this grey fog by giving them love and reassurance, and reminding them of our happy times with them. No matter how people die, they all need love, light and blessings. We must also remember that we shall meet again all those whom we have truly loved.

The power of love to heal, transform and change anything in life is limitless. Elizabeth Kubler Ross, who specialises in death and dying, decided to open her house in Virginia to babies born with AIDS. Most of their mothers were prostitutes who also had AIDS. Fearful of the consequences when their babies were born, they had abandoned them in doorways or on hospital steps. Kubler Ross was prevented from using her house in this way by local people who feared that she was bringing AIDS into the county. Instead, a number of volunteer families took the babies into their own homes for what was presumed would be only a few months until they died. They gave them so much love that they literally loved the babies back to life. Many recovered from the virus and were pronounced completely healthy.

If we ourselves loved our bodies when ill, instead of rejecting them and treating them like an enemy, we would recover more easily. Illness is a message, a communication from the soul. It is a confrontation in the physical of what we are reluctant to deal with mentally or emotionally, and thus a unique opportunity for transformation. However, we also need to remember that ultimate healing is release from the physical body: there is a time to be born and a time to die. No death happens by accident, however we see it from our limited human perspective.

When Plato was on his death-bed, he was asked the key to life. 'Prepare for death,' he replied. We can prepare for death the same way as we prepare for a birth. Simple breathing, relaxation and meditational exercises, together with a periodic review of life, and working on whatever needs to be put right, are all good preparations. We can also use dreams, visualisation, and writing.

Visualising your own death

For example, I can use dreams and visualisation to imagine myself dying easily. It is like a dress rehearsal for the real thing. I could also ask to be shown how I died in another life. If I have a fear of the manner in which I die, such as lying paralysed for months on end after a heart attack, a good way to deal with it is to write as full a description as possible of what this would be like for myself and for my family; how would I feel, and what would I physically experience, and think? I would then burn it. I next describe how I would choose to die, in as much detail as possible. I do not burn this, but tuck it away in a drawer or in my journal. From time to time I re-read it, and sometimes visualise myself dying in the way I have chosen. This ritual, however simple, helps to programme my mind for a happier death.

The more we practise meditation and visualisation and our expansion of consciousness beyond the physical reality which they present, the easier it will be for us to move on. We can help one another make this transition by creating an atmosphere of peace and light around a dying person, instead of the doom, gloom and despondency usual in such cases. Crystals, flowers, candles, sandalwood, soft music, fragrant-smelling herbs, or oils to give a light massage, all help us move our consciousness into the spiritual dimension.

A friend of mine sings to her dying patients, and will often hold them in her arms as they take their last breath. Another friend, a nurse, gently massages their feet and hands, and tells them it is all right for them to go – all they need to do is to follow the light and stay with it until they see a familiar face. Myrtle, a friend who died of cancer two years ago, was taken by her husband Jack to the hospice, only hours before her death. He sat and stroked her hair, and spoke soothingly to her about their life together, even though she was barely conscious. Suddenly, to the surprise of another friend who was also in the room, Jack pulled back the covers and got into bed with Myrtle. For about an hour he held her lovingly, telling her gently it was all right for her to leave him. With a tiny sigh, she died.

Tragically, most of us die desperately alone and uncomforted in a hospital bed, although invisible spiritual help is always present. Future generations will judge our current attitude to death and dying as completely barbaric. However, by then humanity will almost certainly no longer fear death, but see it as an ever-present part of the process of life. In the past ancient peoples saw sleep as a little death, and death as a little sleep. The Essenes prepared for death every night, by leaving nothing undone or unfinished that they might regret if they did not awake the next day. They greeted each morning as if it were the start of a new life.

If enough of us today could also see death as a little sleep, and that we die in order to become new, we could help humanity rid itself of this needless dread. Our minds and imaginations, when joined with hundreds of others, have the energy and power to create deep and lasting change in the world. What happens is what is called critical mass, when a certain number of individuals affect the consciousness of all others.

Death is a metamorphosis – the caterpillar turning into the butterfly. Dying is the process of discarding an outer sheath, like an old coat that imprisons the essence of who we are. Death is freedom from restriction. In the words of Goethe:

'Nature invented death that there might be more abundant life . . . If you have not got this, this concept of death and becoming, you are but a dull guest in a dark world.'

12

INTO THE NEXT MILLENNIUM

. . . We are in a time so strange
That living equals dreaming,
And this teaches me that man
Dreams his life, awake.

CALDERON, *La Vida es Sueño*

Nostradamus's predictions for the end of the millennium

A French doctor who lived in Provence over 400 years ago predicted these 'times so strange' in detail. Nostradamus was his name. Nostradamus was probably one of the greatest mystics and prophets ever known to mankind. In the 1500s he predicted that the end of the millennium would be charged with conflicts and upheavals, earthquakes, global warming, famine, flood, holes in the ozone layer, black holes, space-craft crashes, and AIDS sweeping the Earth 'like a plague of locusts'. Long before their invention he foresaw cars, aero-planes, television, radio, weapons of war, industrial ma-chines, and much of the modern technology we take for granted today. He predicted the use of sound waves to kill cancer, new treatment for old age and senility, and how genetic science would discover the cause of disease rather than merely use drugs to treat its symptoms.

Nostradamus burned all his papers before his death for two reasons. First, he did not want them to fall into the wrong hands. Second, he did not want to frighten the people around him, for the changes he predicted were far more rapid and cataclysmic than anything that had happened in the world before. He then condensed his original prophecies into obscure verses known as quatrains, to prevent future generations also from knowing too much about the changes to come. His predictions cover thousands of years, but their main thrust seemed always the 1990s and the new epoch.

Our impending evolution

I am quite sure that a man of Nostradamus's time who suddenly found himself in the twentieth century would indeed think that 'living equals dreaming', as we might if we could see into the future a few hundred years from now. I have previously described the changes that lie ahead as being as great as when man first came out of the water and walked on land. Perhaps this was more true of the Renaissance man than any other. Today, instead of moving from water to land, we are moving from the Earth into the sky, to inter-planetary exploration and colonisation.

To do this we need to adapt. To survive underwater we need diving equipment. When we step out of the water our wet suits, flippers, goggles and air tanks hinder rather than help us. We remove them quickly. I believe that in a few hundred years man will no longer have the physical body he has today. However amazing and wonderful our bodies may be today, they may be too dense for the new world to which we are even now adapting.

Many years ago during a workshop on male-female relationships, I had a dream in which I saw what the dream described as the sons and daughters of God coming to Earth for the first time. They were sparks of light encased in etheric bodies who came down to the Earth to play. Initially androgynous, these sons and daughters of God projected parts of themselves into rocks, trees, flowers, even animals, to discover what it felt like. Many of them got stuck and forgot their origins, and thus became trapped in matter.

We, their descendants, who also came to Earth to find out what it was like to be spirit encased in matter are now, with planet Earth herself, lifting from matter into spirit. I believe that our future bodies will be light, etheric, and have the same power of projection. Our minds will be clear, light and open. We shall no longer fear death, hunger and thirst, cold or heat. Instead of driving cars or flying in aeroplanes, we shall simply move about the globe by projecting our consciousness to wherever we want to go. Tibetan lamas, Indian sages, medicine men and women from various indigenous tribes have always done this.

The desire to be in a certain place, or spend time with a particular friend, will automatically draw us to them. If we want to know what is happening anywhere in the world, or even on other planets, we shall 'switch on' clairvoyantly and telepathically, exactly as we switch on the radio or television today. Reincarnation, past-life therapy, and the laws of karma or cause and effect, will be accepted not just as a theory, but as a fundamental requirement for self-understanding.

Future education and communication

Our current process of reasoning will appear formal and dead. Intuition and creative imagination will be more important than logic and intelligence. Even today, education is no longer an automatic guarantee of work. The widespread use of computers and advanced technology have already introduced us to the idea that new generations are evolving who will never work in the same way as man did in the past. Ultimately this will dissolve the barriers between the right and the left brain, and push us to identify ourselves with who we are, rather than what we do.

Future children, instead of lessons of reading, writing and arithmetic, will learn how universal laws, such as the Kabbalah, can be applied to any aspect of life, from running an office to building a house. Instead of the current dry, text-book studies of history, they will be shown how to read the Akashic record, and even how to project themselves into past historical events. Their education will include a review of their own past lives, in order that they see and understand the dominant tendencies in them, and correct those felt to be destructive.

They will not be segregated as now by age, but rather by interest. Classes are more likely to take place in gardens and parks, rather than in institutionalised buildings as at present. Students will be encouraged to study the heavens, the sun, the phases of the moon, the movements of the planets, as well as astrology, numerology, palmistry and phrenology. Instead of suffering written exams, they will be guided by astrological and numerological charts to discover the issues or concerns that affect or interest them.

Schools of the future will teach their pupils how to develop their psychic powers and occult wisdom. They will learn how to read the omens, portents and symbols presented in the shifting shapes of clouds, the movement of the wind, the flutter of a butterfly's wing, the patterns in the sand, a feather on the ground, as much as by their study of the occult sciences such as the Tarot.

The Tarot cards come from the occult schools of ancient Egypt. Originally designed to help students learn how to decipher the hieroglyphs which depicted the mysteries of life and death, and how best to adapt to them, they have now become for many a symbol of fortune-telling. When used properly and with reverence, they can be a key for exploration of our sub and unconscious selves. Much of the new teaching will come from discarnate entities, angels and guides.

In Nostradamus's time, this type of communication was called prophecy. In Edgar Cayce's, it was described as a reading. Today we call it channelling. All over the world there are currently hundreds of people claiming to be channels for discarnate entities. These range from your uncle, who died last year – and, however willing to help, no wiser than when he was incarnate – to beings of incredible intelligence and understanding such as Seth, channelled by the late Jane Roberts, who inspired thousands of people internationally to see themselves and life in a different way.

Many others claim connection to star people from the Pleiades or Venus. I believe that the current explosion of channelling is indicative of the dissolving barrier between physical and spiritual worlds. In future 'channelling' will be accepted as completely normal, and invisible teachers as common as university professors.

People of the future will use telepathy and clairvoyance as their means of communication. They will have new accelerated forms of learning, which will include conscious changing of the brain-wave rhythm. Instead of morning prayers, or commands to pay attention, tomorrow's children will probably be guided into a state of deep meditation which will help them absorb information more easily.

Years ago Jose Silva, founder of Silva Mind Control, guided the extremely poor Mexican children he was trying to teach into an altered state of consciousness before he began the day. Because many of them arrived at the school barefoot and hungry, he also got them to imagine eating a large breakfast. Almost immediately, his pupils began to learn better, and even developed a psychic sensitivity which enabled them to know what he was going to say before he said it. His success led him to develop the techniques presented under the title of Silva Mind Control.

Children will be encouraged to seek for knowledge within themselves, rather than just from a teacher, a book, a video or computer. They will refer to intuition for guidance, rather than an outside authority, and learn the language of dreams as naturally as we learn French or German. They will also learn that it is not knowledge that builds the soul, but rather its application to daily life. Their education will draw out of them exactly what they need to fulfil their potential instead of stifling it as much of our education does today.

A very sad example of this is the story of a child in Canada who loved to draw the sun, the sky and vast landscapes with no horizon. His teacher urged him to 'draw planes, trains, cars and houses like Johnny does'. At twelve he committed suicide, after writing a verse to his teacher in which he said he lost all his joy from having to sit at a square desk in a square room, in a square building surrounded by a square playground, draw and write on neat little squares of paper and copy what everyone else did. In the future, children will be encouraged to explore the heights and depths of creation, and freely to express their own individuality. By then, they will probably be androgynous, but will also know that they have occupied both male and female bodies, that neither is superior to the other, but simply offers a different opportunity and experience.

Contacting your guide through meditation

While children of the future may instinctively know how to contact their teachers and guides, how do we go about it today? The answer is meditation. Meditation bypasses the conscious mind and opens us to infinite wisdom and the reality of God and other realms. We are already channellers or mediators for the energy that, in moving through us, enables us to accomplish what we need to do. However, most of us do this unconsciously. To make a conscious connection with a teacher, guide or wisdom beyond our human perception, it is best to prepare a little.

Aside from the breathing and relaxation techniques I described previously, we should wash, and then put on, either in reality or imagination, a garment that signifies the importance of what we are about to do. This will impress on mind, body and spirit that we are about to enter another dimension. We can make this effect all the more realistic if we also imaginatively create a special or sacred place, such as a mountain cave, an island, a temple or a forest glade – whatever may be most meaningful to us in the moment. We should now, with eyes closed, visualise our teacher or guide appearing in front of us, and say to him or her: 'Please, I want to get to know you better. I want to see you, feel you, hear you. I want to know that you are near me, participating in my life.'

Listen to the reply and write it down. Initially we may feel that we are making it up. I know that I thought this myself when, after months of meditation, words poured into my mind which I had no option but to write down. I felt slightly ashamed and even crazy, thinking that this was perhaps the only way in which my subconscious could express itself. Finally, I showed a friend some of the information that 'came through' in this way, and asked if she thought it nonsensical. She roared with laughter, and told me it was far too intelligent for me to have made it up. I began to trust this superior intelligence, but I also questioned it, and asked for proof that this information came from beyond me, rather than from me.

Not knowing just what proof to ask for, I said: 'Speak to me like Noël Coward, Samuel Johnson, Thomas Mann, Charles Dickens, Somerset Maugham ...' The words and language changed instantly, reflecting each writer in a way that I could never have done. This proof was also given to me independently in many forms. For example, a string of words spoken by my guide which I had written down would be repeated to me verbatim by a stranger on a bus, or an astrologer who unexpectedly offered to read my chart. Since then, this guidance has been one of the main factors which have helped me to live my life in a totally different way.

Many people may think it wrong to question what appears to be a deeply spiritual experience, but I believe we should always question its validity. Ultimately, we must learn to trust ourselves, our own authority, develop our own integrity and completeness of being, without dependence on anything or anyone else – whether incarnate or discarnate.

To channel is to listen, to allow something to come through, rather than to push or force something to happen. Our guides may appear in a non-physical form, such as lines of light or colour. For a long time I saw my own guides as little round smiley faces, or yellow boxes each with 'love' written on them, or sometimes hearts cascading out of the ceiling. There is no need to try to force images. It is, rather, better to imagine what it would feel like to be in the presence of a beloved older brother or sister who knew everything about you, completely loved and accepted you, and could advise you on any aspect of life you chose to ask about.

Visualising your Book of Life

It is sometimes helpful to ask your guide for your Book of Life, as a trigger to opening your consciousness to this type of communication. Imagine the colour, size and weight of such a book. In your mind's eye see your name embossed on the cover, feel the paper, thick or thin, leather-bound or not, old or new.

The more you practise this type of exercise, the clearer your answers will be. When you open it, what does its text say? You may not see exact words, but allow whatever impressions emerge to flow into your mind, and write them down. Always remember to say thank you to your guide. The book *God Calling* was written in this way, as were many other books that inspire and help us.

Children of the next millennium will, in their new light bodies, see auras as clearly as we see the physical body today. Knowing that whatever they think and feel will be instantly revealed in the auric field, their education will include aura-cleansing and chakra-balancing.

The chakras

The chakras are seven vital centres that go from the top of the head to the base of the spine. They are like power points where lines of energy meet and cross. The chakras control the organs and glands of the body, and each one relates to a different frequency on the colour scale. The main chakras are:

1 The *root*, at the base of the spine. The related colour is red; the gland is the gonads.
2 The *spleen*, or *sacral* chakra, two to three inches below the navel. The related colour is orange; the gland is the adrenals.
3 The *solar plexus*, at the diaphragm. The related colour is yellow; the gland is the pancreas.
4 The *heart*, mid chest. The related colour is green, the gland is the thymus.
5 The *throat*. The related colour is blue; the gland is the thyroid.
6 The *brow*, or *third eye* in the centre of the forehead. The related colour is indigo; the gland is the pituitary.
7 The *crown* chakra, at the top of the head. The related colour is violet; the gland is the pineal.

There is another centre, whose colour is white, about eighteen inches above the crown, and others including in the knees and feet, but it is more usual to focus on the seven I have just described.

Assessing the health of the chakras

A simple way to assess the health or otherwise of the chakras is to imagine the body as a seven-storey building, and move from basement to roof assessing each floor as we go. On the roof, we can meet the caretaker, and ask if he or she thinks one floor needs more attention than another. A friend of mine who did this discovered that she had a problem when going up in a lift, when she could not get out at the fifth floor –

equivalent to her throat. She suddenly realised that she never said what she really wanted to say, fearing how others might perceive her. When I did this exercise myself, I saw that the walls on the sixth floor were crumbling. I later discovered that I had osteo-arthritis in my jaw.

Balancing the chakras

The flow of energy between the chakras affects our physical health as well as our sense of well-being, so it is a good idea to take care of them. There are a number of ways to balance the chakras, including the use of crystals. One way is to take a 4–5 in. natural quartz crystal pressed firmly against the palm of your right hand, and hold it point down a few inches above each chakra, rotating it both clock- and anti-clockwise, depending on which chakra you are treating.

In a woman, the chakra is anti-clockwise at the crown, clockwise at the brow, anti-clockwise at the throat, clockwise at the heart, anti-clockwise at the solar plexus, clockwise at the spleen, and anti-clockwise at the root. In the man, it is the exact opposite. If you make an anti-clockwise movement on a chakra whose natural flow is clockwise, it can cause discomfort. If you hold a crystal on or near chakras it can also balance them as well as recharge the aura. It does not matter whether you start at the crown or the base, and, although you can do it for yourself, it is more effective if another does it to you.

A good alternative way of balancing the chakras is to imagine white light pouring into each centre from the one above the top of the head. Sit on a chair with your spine straight, or lie down flat, and visualise the light coming through the skull and flowing to each chakra from crown to base. You can also visualise circles or stars of colour glowing on each chakra. When I do this, I prefer to go from base to crown. I find this extra powerful if I chant sound with each colour. As a child, I used to see everything around me as kaleidoscopic waves of sound and colour – music had colour, colour was music. To quote Christopher Hills, founding member of the University of the Trees in America, 'everything in creation is singing its own song'.

The sounds I use are ones I learnt from an amazing spiritual teacher, psychic and metaphysician called William David in America. William used to be an opera singer, and teaches all his students how to work with colour and sound, so that they can each find their own unique soul-song and join in with what is literally the music of the spheres. We chant these sounds of colour in all my workshops. They have a similar effect on our physical bodies, chakras, auras and states of consciousness as do crystals. The more we practise, the more effective they become. The correlation between these colours and sounds is:

- Red   EE   pitch C
- Orange   EH   pitch G
- Yellow   AAH   pitch E
- Green   AY   pitch D
- Blue   OH   pitch B
- Indigo   OM   pitch F
- Violet   OO   pitch A
- White   I AM (meaning I am one with the source of life, the heart, the mind of God)

A quick pick-me-up if we feel distressed by the traumas of these times is to sit in an orange bath – use a few drops of orange cake colouring – and sing EH for twenty to thirty minutes, then wrap ourselves up warmly and go to bed.

Colour therapy

Colour therapy is already widely used to treat many of today's problems. It can range from placing violent criminals or mental patients in pale pink rooms, to electro-crystal treatment which beams colour into specified areas of the diseased or ill body. I recently saw a computer image of a woman which showed a lot of red in her throat. After the treatment, it became blue, and therefore healthy for that area. In the ancient and now sunken city of Atlantis, the priests and priest-esses clairvoyantly saw blocks in the energy system of a person, which indicated disease, which was then treated by colour, crystal lasers (also used in orthodox medicine today) and sound waves, that balanced the inner as well as the outer bodies.

In the world to come, people will probably have the ability to beam sound and colour waves into the ill or indisposed, without recourse to instruments. Meanwhile, we can all improve the quality of our health and our sense of well-being by visualising or wearing the colours we think most beneficial to us.

A colour meditation

A colour meditation I use both for myself and in workshops is to imagine entering different-coloured tents or rooms in a house. Sometimes I simply go into them and think of the colours renewing and revitalising all the organs, cells, muscles and tissues in my body. At other times I use the colours as a means of connection to different aspects of myself.

For example, I might imagine entering a red tent to find my animus or masculine side, a blue tent to find my anima or female side, orange to see who needs forgive-ness, green to find my shadow, yellow to find not only the child of my past but also the pure inner divine child, indigo to look for past lives that may affect my life today, and violet to look for future or even co-existent selves. I finish with a white tent, in which I meet my teacher or dream guide, and ask for information or help, or else I simply imagine myself bathed with light before I open my eyes again.

To get the full benefit of this exercise, it may be better if you record it on a tape and listen to it later. We can visualise entering all the tents one after another in the same thirty to forty minutes, or take one tent a day. Either way, this exercise can bring a lot of insight.

In the 1960s Christopher Hills introduced the idea of creative conflict in which assessment of people by the colour of their personality helped bring about understanding. For example, the yellow intellectual must allow for the red level man to become restless over meticulous and lengthy planning. The red personality man has to accept that the blue may seek an authority-basis for his decisions, while the yellow planner tries to fit everything into a logical framework. The orange person may base what he or she does on a sense of approval or disapproval from those around him or her.

Every soul comes into incarnation on one of seven rays, which Alice Bailey, the great Theosophist, described in detail in her many books. Each ray has a different vibration and colour, and produces a different psychological type. Christopher Hills's work is another way of looking at the same thing. Today we may assess what colour a person is from the way he or she behaves. The people of tomorrow will immediately understand another person's behaviour or attitude by seeing what ray they incarnated on, and the colours predominant in the aura.

Aura cleansing exercises

Auric colours can change, depending on what we are doing or how we are feeling. The more physical we are, the more dense the colours, the more spiritually awake, the lighter and more etheric the colours will be. Children of the future will cleanse their auras as automatically as the children of today clean their teeth. The following method is one I use myself every morning when I wake up and every night before I go to bed. If I feel at all wobbly during the day, I do it then too.

I shake my hands in front of me as if I were shaking off drops of water, and in doing so re-charge my electro-magnetic field. I put my forefingers and index fingers on my brow, then pull them down over my cheeks to under my jaw, and shake my hands off again. Next, I cup my hands under my chin, and lift my linked hands over the top of my head and down to the back of my neck, and shake my hands off in front of me again. I do this last complete movement three times.

I follow this by putting my right hand across to my left shoulder, then brushing down through my auric field to my feet, repeating the same with my left hand to my right shoulder, and down. Next, I put my hands behind me at the small of my back, and brush straight down to my heels, ending by bringing my hands low in front of me, and shaking them off. Finally, I cup my hands in front of my chest, then lift them over my head to the back of my neck, and bring them forward to brush down all the way to my toes, and shaking the crumbs of impurity off my hands to be transformed by God's light.

We can also practise radiating light or colour into the aura from the solar plexus as if we had swallowed the sun, in order to strengthen the aura. After this exercise, I always invoke the presence of the Archangels Michael, Gabriel, Uriel and Raphael for my support and protection, and seal off my aura by imagining myself within a five-pointed star.

Balancing your male and female sides

A visualisation exercise that I enjoy doing from time to time, which puts me in touch with how balanced or not my male and female sides are, is as follows: I make myself comfortable, take a few deep breaths and relax. With my eyes closed, I imagine the left side of my brain, the feel and colour of it, whether it is free and open or tight and restricted. The left brain is the logical or masculine side, the right brain the intuitive, imaginative or feminine side. The left brain controls the right side of the body, the right brain controls the left.

Thus symbolically the left is generally considered

feminine, and the right masculine. I then visualise my right brain, and compare the two sides, which can sometimes appear to be very different. I am usually more comfortable in my right brain. In the same way, I now imagine the left and right halves of my body. I move from one to the other, and sense which in the moment is stronger or weaker.

I then imagine holding a symbol for my male energy in my right hand, and for my female in my left, and again sense which is stronger or weaker, lighter or heavier. I cup my hands, palms upwards, on my lap, and again compare the two before absorbing them into my solar plexus. I then flood my body from top to toe with either light or colour, blending and harmonising both left and right, male and female halves.

This exercise can not only help us to assess the pre-dominance of male/female, and bring them into balance, but also helps to dissolve the barriers between left and right hemispheres of the brain. Another form of this exercise is to stare at your own face in a mirror, covering first the left side, then the right with an A4 sheet of paper. Next, you assess whether the left eye is more open or closed than the right, the eyebrow thicker, thinner, higher or lower, and examine the shape of the cheek, nostril, the droop of the mouth, and again compare left and right, and assess their balance. This is an interesting exercise to do with a partner, and also with the well-known faces of people such as politicians. Our faces symbolise our identities, and reveal how comfortable or uncomfortable we are with our masculine and feminine aspects.

Brain expansion exercise

To do this as a brain-expanding exercise, rather than an assessment of male and female, simply visualise different things happening in each hemisphere of the brain. For example, imagine nails scraping down a blackboard in the left, the sharp, sour taste of a freshly cut lemon in the right, the sound of the sea in the left, glass breaking in the right, a baby crying in the left, a woman screaming in the right, the fragrance of perfume or wild flowers in the left, the smell of freshly ground coffee or badly burnt toast in the right – or anything else that can vividly conjure up taste, sight or sound that stimulate both left and right hemispheres.

The coming spiritual age

Tomorrow's focus will be on spiritual rather than worldly developments. Most orthodox religions today separate man from God, and have deteriorated into meaningless sets of rules and regulations in which the original spirit of truth has become cloaked in dogma. These rules repress and punish impersonally, and control rather than uplift. True spirituality is light, expansive, humorous, not fearsome and restrictive. It is alive with love, laughter, joy, fun and celebration.

To understand the spirit of God, we have to open our hearts to a love beyond human comprehension. We can do this anywhere, and often more easily in the simple surroundings of a garden, a beach, or even our own beds at home, rather than within the cold stone walls of a church or temple. Religious rites were meant to free, not imprison us, and in the future will do just that, by reminding us of the sacred, and that the spirit world and this interact, that we are part of an intelligence that permeates the universe. In the words of Alexander Pope, we shall know 'All are but parts of one stupendous whole, whose body nature is, and God the soul.'

As the barriers dissolve between spirit and matter, as modern physics merges with ancient philosophic ideas, and science proves what religion discovered through faith, co-operation between disciplines rather than competition will become the rule rather than the exception. When reincarnation is accepted as a fact of life rather than a whimsical theory of New Age mystics, people will surely stop polluting the planet. They will help to create a better future world, knowing that they will return to it.

Past-life therapy

According to Dr Ian Stevenson, a psychiatrist who has devoted sixty years of his life to the study of and research into men and women who claim memory of other lives, we are on the brink of proving reincarnation to be an irrefutable truth. He said that during his initial years of research he did not believe that we return to this Earth again and again. He now says that the evidence that we do is too compelling for us to doubt it.

My individual counselling sessions always include regressions into other lives. Even people who doubt the validity of reincarnation have been surprised at the memories that come up which help them to release physical pain or ill health, heal relationships and understand themselves and others better. To re-live a past life is to relieve the emotion or trauma left over from it – although of course many past-life memories are happy. When I walk into a room I often see people dressed in the clothes of other lives, both past and future. It is as if these lives are occurring simultaneously, and so when we heal and change a negative aspect of one life, this automatically affects the others.

Past-life therapy exercises

Past-life therapy is already accepted today by many doctors and psychologists as a means of discovering the cause of a problem rather than treating its symptoms. Deep-seated problems are better sorted out with the help of a therapist. However, a simple way to begin is to sit comfortably, breathe and relax, and then imagine facing and going through in turn three doors. One is the door to the past, another to the present, and the third to the future.

Initially, in your mind's eye, compare all three, their shape, colour and size, and to which you feel most drawn to open first. Before going through the door to the past, you might ask to be shown either another life that may be impinging on the current one, or a time in this life that needs healing or resolving. Ask to be shown clearly what from the past of this or another life is affecting you today, what you need to focus more attention on or release altogether in the present, and what qualities from future or co-existent selves you can draw into your life today.

At the end, blend these images together, and merge with them, knowing that they will then become part of your soul's wisdom, and that their energy will co-operate with rather than fight against you.

A different way to get in touch with another life is to focus on a person, country, piece of music, literature or history, that for some reason feels familiar and comfortable. Having gone through the preliminary breathing and relaxation techniques, close your eyes and mentally say: 'Where did I know you before?' Concentrate on the person or place and keep repeating the question until the answer comes. You might want to imagine drifting down into the past, floating through a blue mist which gradually clears, enabling you to see what is there. If you find that there is something unfinished, use your imagination to complete it, visualise a new outcome, heal, forgive or release the personality you discover. If it is yourself, integrate with it before opening your eyes.

Past lives and karma

As we begin to understand and clear old karma – what we have set in motion for ourselves from one life to another – we become more self-reliant and responsible. Karma is really a refining of ourselves. Each lifetime provides myriad experiences through which we can grow and learn, and for many this current life is one in which we can clear the karma of every other. In past epochs, we had time to deal with the results of what we created. As the planetary vibratory rate increases, we are dealing with instant manifestations or immediate karma. For example, my next-door neighbour, without permission, cut down a tree in our garden and was baffled by my reaction. About three hours later, another neighbour cut down one of the first neighbour's trees, and my first neighbour was outraged. This is instant karma.

Many of us today are reincarnating into another life without actually leaving our physical bodies. We sense the Wei Chi time of death and birth. It is the death of limitation and of the false identity, and a birth into a world vastly different from anything we have experienced before. A new baby cries a lot, sleeps a lot, and, away from the comfort and safety of his mother's womb, no doubt feels as if it has been thrown out of home before it is ready, and is vulnerable in what is initially an alien world. Many of us cry a lot, sleep a lot, and feel just as vulnerable, as we awaken to new life in this coming epoch. All the exercises that remind us that we have been here many times, played many parts, and do not have to carry the unnecessary baggage of our pasts around with us any more, help trigger our consciousness to leap into the unknown with excitement rather than fear.

Focusing on priorities

Visualisation is not the only way to heal ourselves, but is a road to expand our consciousness into higher dimensions, and literally helps us bridge the gap between our physical and spiritual senses. Aside from the myriad forms of inner work available to us, we can also help to bridge this gap by our style of life, one aspect of which is to allow ourselves time to do what we most love to do. Most of us are so busy trying to survive that we are not fully alive. We need to focus on our true priorities, simplify our lives, and drop what is unimportant.

There is a story of a monk who spent seventy years of his life trying to levitate to impress his Master. He finally flew across a lake and landed at his Master's feet, exclaiming: 'I can fly! I can fly!' The Master replied: 'Why did you waste so much time on levitation when you could easily have caught the boat?' What do *we* waste our time on which is not really necessary?

Detoxifying our bodies

We should get our priorities right as concerns our health and diet too. We can eat fresh, live food, lots of fruit, vegetables, nuts and pulses, rather than overload our bodies with the toxicity that comes from too much dead meat and processed food. Years ago, I became a vegetarian, and for two years lived entirely on raw food. I felt better and had more energy than at any other time in my life. I now eat fish and cooked vegetables, but still like to eat a lot of raw food. This diet may not suit everyone, but certainly improves my own lightness of being.

To clear the body of toxicity   Drink at least eight glasses of water a day, and try to do an occasional three-day fast. If you feel that you will not survive on no food at all, do a three-day grape, apple or water-melon fast. This means eating the same food all the time, and no tea, coffee or alcohol. Alternatively, try a once-a-week fast, eating your lunch one day, then nothing until the evening of the next day. After fasting, especially for three days, your mind will feel crystal-clear and your body light, and the first food you eat will taste like the nectar of the gods.

Breathing exercise

Beinsa Douna instructed his students to walk every day, preferably away from the smoke and dust of the city, and to practise breathing and physical exercises daily. Ten to fifteen minutes of the following exercise will improve the quality of our breathing as well as our attitude to the day.

Stand with your feet shoulders' width apart, slowly inhale and open your arms wide. Hold your breath, then slowly bring your arms forward and upwards, palms touching before exhaling. Repeat as many times as you can. Even if we can only do exercises in our own houses or apartments rather than outside, the benefits can be life-changing.

Greeting the sun

Beinsa Douna also taught his students to greet the sun at dawn and sunset, rather as did the Essenes. The Hopi Indians greet the morning sun with this prayer:

> *I ask that this day*
> *The Sky Father and Earth Mother*
> *Meet in my heart,*
> *That they will be inseparable*
> *Today and for ever more. HO!*

A new perspective

To go to the mountains or climb the nearest hill can also give us a new perspective in the same way as can meditation. Beinsa Douna said that one of the most helpful practices for a healthy life was to go to the mountains for as long as possible at least once a year. In this way our spirits can meet and greet spirits descending from above.

A harmonious environment

In Africa, a man I know built new houses for the workers on his father's farm. They were square bungalows with modern kitchens and bathrooms. With great excitement, the workers moved in. Six months later they all moved back to their round mud huts, saying that they were losing their souls in square houses and with tiled floors separating their feet from the ground. Black Elk made a similar statement about the native

American Indians after the whites put them into square houses.

We may not all be able to live in round houses, but we can arrange our possessions in such a way that energy circulates smoothly, and people feel comfortable and revitalised. In the orient this 'art of placement' is called Feng Shui. Feng Shui takes years of study and practice. It is based on the recognition of the invisible energy flowing through all space and form, and how best to use it to create harmony.

In China, Feng Shui experts are often called in to advise on the exterior and interior design of new buildings, and harmoniously to realign the interiors of existing buildings, including homes, in order to bring good fortune to those working or living within them. Because this skilled and intuitive shaping of our surroundings can have so great an influence upon our health and happiness, it is certainly well worth our while to apply Feng Shui to our own lives.

Alignment with the Tao

Feng Shui, which means 'wind-water', can help us live in alignment with the Tao. Alignment with the Tao means that everything falls into place for us, and life is no longer a constant battle. Inner and outer realms, conscious and unconscious, begin to work together. Jung's theory of synchronicity is in harmony with the Tao. For example, while writing this book, I could not locate the girl who agreed to type for me. After fifteen phone calls, I began to feel a little desperate. Suddenly the daughter of a friend appeared on my doorstep and asked if I had any typing to be done.

Again while preparing this book, I had just written a few words on Nostradamus when someone switched on the radio, and I heard, uncannily, almost word for word what I had just put down. On another occasion, I needed urgently to go shopping, but did not want to interrupt my work. Astoundingly, a friend walked into the kitchen with a huge basket of fruit and vegetables from a local farm. These synchronicities are happening more and more frequently for all of us.

George Bernard Shaw described the world we are rapidly moving into with these words: 'The visible world is not the only reality, and the invisible no longer a dream.' This blending of visible and invisible means that logic on its own does not work any more. If we try to do things in the old ways, there will either be no energy, or what we thought we ought to do will be interrupted by something totally different. We have to move from masculine to feminine, stop thinking, pushing, doing, and relax into feeling, listening, being and allowing. If we can do this the energy flows.

We who are of the twentieth to twenty-first century are crossing the boundaries between the known and unknown; there are no maps, there is no framework, we are moving into uncharted territory. We have to adapt to living in the middle of a hologram, where anything is possible, a quantum space of miracles and magic. We must remember that even if we do not consciously know how to take the next step the soul-essence of who we are contains the blueprint of what we came here to do and to be. We were born ready, with the answers within us. We have to start living from soul-essence, not just personality, from the intuition and inspiration of the heart, not of the mind.

The magic of living in the centre of a hologram, or to be aligned with the Tao, means that we do more by doing less. We picture and imagine every facet of what we want to accomplish first. If I write a book, I do not just sit down and start to type, but rather visualise for whom I am writing, and why; who will edit, print, publish and distribute this book; which country will the ink, trees and paper come from; who will cut the trees down, and so on.

From the centre of the hologram I create the whole picture, which allows the energy to flow, moves me into a different vibration, which draws to me everything I need to help this project without effort. This approach reminds us that we have inside us all the tools we need to accomplish or be whatever we want, that we can call on resources we have never called on before.

Visualising our own essence

To find and use our essence, we should simply imagine it forming at the top of our heads until it becomes so clear to our inner eye that we could almost touch it. Breathe it, through the chakras, into the solar plexus, and allow it to flow into whatever we want to do.

We have a responsibility to express ourselves, and the power to do so, as we have never had before. To understand what is happening now, we have to develop our spiritual senses, which may lead us to say: 'I do not understand, but I'm willing to create a space for the understanding to come in.' This is the difference between being and doing – it allows.

We may discover that our sole purpose in life is to express love. At the end of World War II a psychiatrist, entering a concentration camp to assess the health and psychological balance of the prisoners, met a man who was so radiantly healthy that he assumed him to be an informer, or recently captured. When questioned, the man said: 'I had the option to make the best or worst of the situation I was in. I decided to love everyone around me, captors and prisoners alike.'

By doing this, he not only affected everyone around him, but also himself. We can do the same today, by calling on our essence to hold everything and everyone around us in light. Simply picture them whole, healthy and happy. If we doubt our ability to make a difference, we can visualise drawing a sword of power from a rock, rather as King Arthur did with Excalibur. We must then claim the power that is rightfully ours and which is the sum total of all the experiences in all the lives that we have ever had.

Invoking the light of your love

The current universe cannot be understood rationally. Thinking about problems simply reinforces them. By opening our hearts, and using to the full the power of the imagination, we can catalyse enormous change.

Let us close our eyes for a moment, and imagine the flame of a candle inside our hearts. Let us feel it, imagine it getting bigger and bigger, and expanding to fill our entire bodies. The flame of our hearts reaches out, threads and streams of light, filigree threads of light, stream towards the members of our families, then into the hearts and minds of presidents and prime ministers, starving children in Africa and Bosnia, repressed people world-wide.

Imagine threads of light going out and out, connecting us with trees, flowers, the Earth, stones, hills, valleys, seas and lakes, with oceans, suns and moons. For a moment, let us be aware of life and light breathing us, not us breathing them. Let us breathe in joy and laughter, and let it out, breathe in sadness, sorrow, breathe it out. Imagine the whole planet suffused in the light of your love.

Awakening to change means that now the human heart can go the lengths of God. We have that power.

> *The human heart can go the lengths of God.*
> *Dark and cold we may be, but this*
> *Is no winter now. The frozen misery*
> *Of centuries breaks, cracks, begins to move.*
> *The thunder is the thunder of the floes,*
> *The thaw, the flood, the upstart spring.*
> *Thank God our time is now, when wrong*
> *Comes up to face us everywhere,*
> *Never to leave us till we take*
> *The longest stride of soul men ever took.*
> *Affairs are now soul size.*
> *The enterprise is exploration into God.*
> *Where are you making for? It takes*
> *So many thousand years to wake,*
> *But will you wake for pity's sake?*

CHRISTOPHER FRY, *The Sleep of Prisoners*

FURTHER READING

Alder, Vera Stanley *Finding the Third Eye, The Atomic Age, The 5th Dimension* (Rider)

Bach, Richard *Illusions, Jonathan Livingston Seagull, One, The Gift of Living* (Pan)

Bailey, Alice *Esoteric Astrology I & II, Esoteric Healing, Esoteric Psychology I & II, Glamour: A World Problem, Initiation: Human and Solar, The 7 Rays, Treatis on White Magic, Unfinished Biography* (Lucis Trust)

Brunton Paul *A Search in Secret India, A Secret Path, Secret Search in Egypt, The Hidden Teachings Beyond Yoga* (Rider)

Campbell, Joseph *Myths to Live by, The Masks of God* (Penguin)

Cayce, Edgar *Edgar Cayce on Atlantis, Edgar Cayce on Reincarnation, Edgar Cayce's Story of Jesus, Edgar Cayce's Story of Karma* (Bantam)

Carey, Ken *Vision* (Starseed)

Colton, Ann Ree *Watch Your Dreams* (ARC)

Diamond, Harvey and Marilyn *Fit for Life* (Bantam)

Fortune, Dion *Sane Occultism* (Aquarian)

Gurdjieff *Views from the Real World* (Arkana)

Haiche, Elizabeth *Initiation* George Allen and Unwin

Jung, Carl *Man and His Symbols* (Pan), *Memories, Dreams and Reflections* (Fontana)

Montgomery, Ruth *A Search for the Truth, A World Beyond* (Futura) *Born to Heal* (J.K. Hall)

Ouspensky & Schroeder *A New Model of the Universe, In Search of the Miraculous, Tertium Organum, The Fourth Way* (Arkana)

Spalding, Baird T. *Life and Teachings of the Masters of the Far East* (Devorss)

Watson, Lyall *The Romeo Error, Supernature* (Hodder and Stoughton)

Watts, Alan *The Wisdom of Insecurity* (Rider)

Wilson, Colin *The Occult: A History* (Hodder and Stoughton)

Yogananda *Autobiography of a Yogi* (Rider)

USEFUL ADDRESSES

Roy Gillett
32 Glynswood
Camberley
Surrey GU15 1HU

For Soozi Holbeche workshops contact:

Maggie Roberts
260 Kew Road
Richmond
Surrey TW9 3EQ

For Soozi Holbeche or Paul Solomon tapes
contact:

P.O. Box 23
Yateley
Camberley
Surrey GU17 7DW

INDEX

Aboriginals, 56, 77, 85, 90, 109
acid rain, 100–1
adrenalin, 37
affirmations, 139
agate, 79, 82
AIDS, 34, 147, 148, 151
Akashic record, 90, 154
allergies, 35
American Indians, 52–5, 77, 90, 109, 171–2
American Revolution, 44
amethyst, 79
animal spirits, 110
Antares, 46
Aquarian Age, 12, 112
Arguelles, Jose, 55
astrology, 44–6
Atlantis, 49–50, 51–2, 57, 162
Auden, W.H., 45
auras, 77–8, 80, 158, 163–4
aventurine, 82

babies, 33
Bacon, Francis, 50
Bailey, Alice, 14, 163
Baker, Richard St Barbe, 103

BBC, 86–7
beliefs, 69–70, 71–2
Bellamy, David, 100–1, 102, 108, 109
Bermuda Triangle, 51
Bible, 57, 88
Black Elk, 171–2
blue crystals, 82
Book of Life, 158
Book of Revelation, 46, 57
Bradshaw, John, 30–1
brain, 66, 67–8, 83–4, 89, 91, 155, 164–5
Brantner, John, 147
breathing, 63, 170–1
Brilliant, Ashleigh, 41
Buddha, 56
Buffon, Comte de, 50

Caddy, Peter and Eileen, 8–9, 22
Caldicott, Helen, 101, 108
Canada, 54
cancer, 34
Capricorn, 44–5, 83
cars, 100
Cayce, Edgar, 3, 50–1, 77, 90, 99, 154

Chadwick, Alan, 110
chakras, 24–5, 80, 82, 84, 159–60
channelling, 154–5, 158
Cherokee Indians, 3, 52, 54–5
child, inner, 128–32, 139
childhood, mapping out, 138–9
children, 33, 98, 108–9, 125, 127–8, 154–6, 158
Clark, Dave, 114–5
climate change, 50, 111
clothes, 35
colour, 160–3
conception, 33
consciousness, 114, 118–9
cooking, 110
Copernicus, Nicolas, 5
Cosmic Rooster, year of, 44–5
Cousins, Norman, 21
crucifixion, 38–9
crystal water, 77–9
crystals, 50, 51, 55, 73, 76–87, 88, 160

Daniken, Erich von, 56

David, William, 161
death, 143 – 50
diaries, 136 – 8
dinosaurs, 50, 115
disease, 34, 148
Dogon tribe, 54
Douna, Beinsa (Peter
   Deunov), 23, 111 – 12,
   170 – 1
dreams, 86, 88 – 99,
   136 – 7

ecological crisis, 100 – 3,
   108 – 10
Edison, Thomas, 113,
   114
education, 153 – 6, 158
Einstein, Albert, 113,
   114
electricity, 75 – 6
elestials, 85
emotions, 35 – 6, 37,
   70 – 1
energy, 30, 80 – 1
essence, visualising, 174
Essenes, 103, 118 – 20,
   150, 171
The Evening Standard,
   57
expectations, 72 – 3
exposure, dreams of, 97
extra-terrestrials, 50,
   51 – 2, 56 – 7

fasting, 170
fear, 127
fear of dying, 143 – 7
female side, balancing,
   164 – 5
Feng Shui, 172
Festival for Mind, Body
   and Spirit, 20 – 1
Findhorn Community,
   8 – 9, 20, 22
flood myths, 50, 53
fluorite, tri-coloured, 83
food, 110
forgetfulness, 35 – 6, 43
forgiveness, 139 – 43
Fortune, Dion, 146
Fox, Emmet, 25 – 6
French Revolution, 44
Freud, Sigmund, 90

Fry, Christopher, 175 – 6

Gaia, 111
Germany, 54
Gibran, Khalil, 128, 145
Gillett, Roy, 45 – 6
Goethe, Johann
   Wolfgang von, 150
Great Invocation, 117
green crystals, 82
gremlins, 43
guides, 156 – 8
guilt, 126 – 7
guru-teachers, 5 – 7

Happold, F.C., 9 – 10
Harmonic Convergence,
   55 – 6
Hauy, Abbé, 88
headaches, 112
healing, 67 – 8, 77 – 81,
   104
Herkimer diamonds,
   81 – 2
Hills, Christopher, 114,
   160 – 1, 163
homeopathy, 69
homosexuality, 29, 30 – 1
honouring the Earth,
   106 – 10
Hopi Indians, 52 – 4, 171
Houston, Jean, 15, 113

Ice Ages, 53
imagination, 64 – 5, 131,
   153
immune system, 34
Industrial Revolution, 44
inner child, 128 – 32, 139
insecurity, 39 – 40, 70 – 1
insomnia, 35 – 6
instant manifestation,
   42 – 3

jade, 82
Japan, 54
Jesus Christ, 56, 57, 88
Jones, Clifford, 79
Jones, Jim, 4
journal writing, 136 – 8
Jung, Carl Gustav, 42,
   87, 95, 99, 172

karma, 43, 168 – 9
Kathongua, Dan, 52
Kekulé, 90
kinesiology, 35, 68, 80
Kirlian photography, 80
Krishnamurti, 5 – 6
Kubler Ross, Elizabeth,
   14, 148
kunzite, pink, 84

lapis lazuli, 82
Law of One, 49
Lemuria, 49, 50
Los Angeles, 103 – 4
Love, 31 – 2, 124 – 8
low frequency vibration
   (LVF), 80
Lowen, Alan, 15 – 16, 17

Maclean, Dorothy, 8, 9
Maitreya, 56
malachite, 82
male side, balancing,
   164 – 5
manifestation, instant,
   42 – 3
Mary Magdalene, 105
Matthews, Arthur
   Henry, 56 – 7
Mayan calendar, 3,
   55 – 6
Mead, Margaret, 68 – 9
meat, 110
meditation, 13, 62 – 6,
   155, 156 – 8, 162
migraine, 112
Mohammed, Prophet, 88
Monroe, Marilyn, 126
Montaigne, Michel
   Eyquem de, 50
Moses, 88
Mother Earth, 52, 77,
   111
mountains, 171
Muktenanda, 21
muscle-testing, 35, 68
music, 65, 160 – 1
Muslims, 110
Mystery Schools, 136
myths, 51 – 5

Near Death Experiences
   (NDEs), 140 – 1, 142,
   144 – 5, 146, 147

Neptune, 44–5, 83
New Age, 7–8
New York, 48–9, 52
niacin, 93
nightmares, 94–6
Noah's Ark, 53
Nostradamus, 12, 151–2, 154, 172
nuclear evolution, 114–15
numerology, 45

Olivier, Laurence, 114–15
oxygen, 103

parents, 32–3, 125, 128
past-life therapy, 167–9
patriarchy, 15–17
Paul, St, 46
perceptions, thoughts change, 73
Peter, St, 88
piezoelectricity, 76
Pilgrim, Peace, 70
planetary alignments, 45–6
Plato, 49–50, 123–4, 148
Pleiades, 56, 155
Pluto, 41–2, 46, 83
pollution, 34, 100–1, 111
Pope, Alexander, 166
Porritt, Jonathan, 108, 113
Poseida, 49
prayers, 117, 140
pregnancy, 98
prophecies, 52–5, 106–8, 151–2, 154
psychics, 75–6
pyroelectricity, 76

quantum physics, 76, 89
quartz, 76, 78–80, 81–2

Rabanne, Paco, 51–2
rainbow crystals, 86
Rajneesh, 21
reality, 73, 123–4
rebirth, 41

reincarnation, 167–9
relationships, 28, 31–2, 143
religions, 125–6, 166
Rifkin, Jeremy, 101–2, 108
Roberts, Jane, 155
Rolling Thunder, 52
rose quartz, 79–80
rutilated quartz, 83

Sai Baba, 21
St Beaume, 105–6
Schweitzer, Albert, 145
Scorpion, 46
Seattle, Chief, 106–8
self-healed crystals, 84–5
self-worth, 33, 124–8
Selye, Hans, 21, 103
sensationalism, 37
Seth, 155
sexuality, 29–31
Shamans, 61
Shattock, Admiral, 21
Shaw, George Bernard, 173
Silva, José, 155
Sioux people, 116
Sirius, 54
Skylab Space Laboratory, 53
sleep, 91–2
smokey quartz, 83
sodalite, 82
solar eclipses, 46
solar plexus, 164
Solomon, Paul, 21, 113, 127, 137
Solon, 49
space visitors, 50, 51–2, 56–7
spiritual growth, 32, 38–41, 142
Sri Lanka, 14
'Star Fire Group', 46
Star People, 52, 54, 56, 155
Steno, Nicolaus, 88
Stevens, Isaac I., 106–8
Stevenson, Dr Ian, 167
stress, 80
sugalite, 82, 84
suicide, 147

sun, greeting, 171
Sun Bear, 12, 26
swastika, 54
synchronicity, 42–3, 172–3
Szekely, Edmond Bordeaux, 118–19

TAIOWA, 53
Talmud, 89
Tao, 172, 173
Tarot cards, 154
TB (tuberculosis), 34
Teresa, St, 113–14
Tesla, Nikola, 56–7, 113, 114
thoughts: controlling, 69–72; and electricity, 75–6; power of, 66–9, 114–18; thoughts change perceptions, 73
time, loss of, 27–8
'toxic shame', 30–1
toxins, 170
trees, 103–6
Trevelyan, Sir George, 7–8, 20
True White Brother, 53

United Nations, 48, 54
Uranus, 44–5, 83
Velikovsky, 56
Venus, 57, 155
visualisation, 66, 115–17, 130–5, 136, 142–3, 148–9, 157, 158, 164–6, 169
vitamin B6, 93
Vogel, Marcel, 73, 77
Voltaire, 49–50

water, 77–9, 111–12, 170
watermelon tourmaline, 83
Wilson, Graham, 20
World War II, 54
Wrekin Trust, 20, 21

Yogananda, 6
Ywahoo, Dhyani, 54–5